SPITFIRE II
THE CANADIANS

High Flight

Oh! I have slipped the surly bonds of earth

    And danced the skies on laughter-silvered wings;

Sunward I've climbed, and joined the tumbling mirth

    Of sun-split clouds—and done a hundred things

You have not dreamed of—wheeled and soared and swung

    High in the sunlit silence. hov'ring there

I've chased the shouting wind along, and flung

    My eager craft through footless halls of air.

Up, up the long, delirious, burning blue

    I've topped the windswept eights with easy grace

Where never lark, nor even eagle flew—

    And, while with silent lifting mind I've trod

The high untrespassed sanctity of space

    Put out my hand touched the face of God.

— *JOHN GILLESPIE MAGEE JR.*

412 SQUADRON

Opposite: Poet and pilot John Gillespie Magee with one of the aircraft he flew, VZ-B "Brunhilde," AD 329. His assigned aircraft was another Spitfire V, VZ-H, AD 291, in 412 Squadron, RCAF. — Photo Credit D-Hist, via Steve Fochuk

SPITFIRE II

THE CANADIANS

Robert Bracken

Foreword by James F. "Stocky" Edwards

Artwork by Ron Lowry

The BOSTON
MILLS PRESS

To Dorothée,
who makes many things possible.

Cataloguing in Publication Data

Bracken, Robert, 1950–
    Spitfire II : the Canadians

ISBN 1-55046-267-9

1. Spitfire (Fighter planes).
2. World War, 1939–1945 – Aerial operations, Canadian.
3. World War, 1939–1945 – Personal narratives, Canadian.
I. Lowry, Ron, 1955–   . II. Title.

D792.C2B73 1999   940.54'4971   C99-931859-4

Design and page composition by
Jonathan Freeman, Andrew Smith Graphics Inc.

Printed in Canada

Canada

THE CANADA COUNCIL | LE CONSEIL DES ARTS
FOR THE ARTS | DU CANADA
SINCE 1957 | DEPUIS 1957

We acknowledge for their financial support of our publishing
program the Canada Council, the Ontario Arts Council, and
the Government of Canada through the Book Publishing
Industry Development Program (BPIDP).

Published in 1999 by Boston Mills Press
132 Main Street, Erin, Ontario N0B 1T0
Tel 519-833-2407 Fax 519-833-2195
e-mail books@boston-mills.on.ca
www.boston-mills.on.ca

An affiliate of Stoddart Publishing Co. Limited
34 Lesmill Road, Toronto, Ontario, Canada M3B 2T6
Tel 416-445-3333 Fax 416-445-5967
e-mail gdsinc@genpub.com

Distributed in Canada by
General Distribution Services Limited
325 Humber College Boulevard
Toronto, Canada M9W 7C3
Orders 1-800-387-0141 Ontario & Quebec
Orders 1-800-387-0172 NW Ontario & Other Provinces
e-mail customer.service@ccmailgw.genpub.com
EDI Canadian Telebook S1150391

Distributed in the United States by
General Distribution Services Inc.
85 River Rock Drive, Suite 202
Buffalo, New York 14207-2170
Toll-free 1-800-805-1083
Toll-free fax 1-800-481-6207
e-mail gdsinc@genpub.com
www.genpub.com
PUBNET 6307949

Back cover photo: *This extremely rare wartime colour photo of a 421 Squadron RCAF Spitfire XVI, coded AU-H,*
serial SM 309, was taken March 15, 1945, at Petit Brogel, B-90. — Canadian Forces REC89-1482

This version of the Spitfire replaced the Mk IXs that the squadron had been flying, the main difference being the
installation of American-built Packard Merlin engines. SM 309 was among the first of the new version delivered to
421 Squadron and would serve with that squadron until the end of the war. It was flown by quite a few different
pilots in 421. In January 1945, it was flown mainly by F/O Bill Marshall. In February 1945, it was also flown
extensively by F/O Bill Harper. At the time this photo was taken, in March 1945, it was again flown by F/O Bill
Marshall. In fact, on the day this photo was taken, Bill Marshall had flown SM 309 on a fighter recce mission over
Rheine/Hamm and had been lucky to return, owing to a rare case of engine trouble.

In April 1945, Bill Marshall went to 443 Squadron. SM 309 became Richard "Hap" Beall's aircraft, and was
named "Panama Bound." While a member of the RCAF in 421 Squadron, Richard hailed from the Panama Canal
Zone.

The Spitfire in the National Air Museum, Rockcliffe, Ottawa, is painted as AU-H, and thus looks very similar to
SM 309.

CONTENTS

FOREWORD

Wing Commander James F. "Stocky" Edwards, DFC, DFM

THE AUTHOR, ROBERT BRACKEN, deserves a lot of credit for his books about Spitfires. Many of the books written about Spitfires and fighter pilots scarcely mention the Canadians.

The author's many years of Canada-wide research, interviews with veteran Spitfire pilots, and extensive use of the pilots' photographs and personal memories, leave no doubt that the Canadians were there in their Spitfires during World War II.

They flew Spitfires in RAF fighter squadrons in every theatre of war, including the Far East, Middle East, Malta and Italy. They flew Spitfires in over a dozen RCAF fighter squadrons. Canadian Spitfire pilots were among the best in the Allied forces. It was an aircraft that seemed made for

Wing Commander James E. "Stocky" Edwards, DFC, DFM, with his personal Spitfire XVI, TD 147, marked with his initials. This photograph was taken near the end of the war, when he was commanding officer of 127 Wing RCAF. — RCAF official photo PL 45184

Canadians — it matched their confident and aggressive spirit.

My air force career began when I completed senior matriculation at St. Thomas College, Battleford, Saskatchewan, and hitch-hiked to Saskatoon to enlist in the RCAF. I was called up in October 1940, took my elementary flying training in Edmonton, and then went on to Yorkton, where I received my pilot's wings.

I went overseas in July 1941, and took my OTU at Usworth, on Hurricanes. Along with many other Canadians, I was sent to the Middle East in November 1941, where I would fly in RAF squadrons for the next three years.

I was posted to 94 Squadron in the Western Desert near Tobruk, a squadron which soon afterwards converted from Hurricanes to Kittyhawks. I shot down my first Messerschmitt 109 on my first operational sortie. In May 1942 I joined 260 RAF Squadron, flying Kittyhawks, and for the next

twelve months the squadron flew in close support of the Eighth Army, strafing, dive-bombing and bomber escorting.

It was usually the Me 109s that attacked our formations. Of the 400 RCAF fighter pilots who flew on RAF squadrons in the Middle East, more than a third were shot down by Me 109s. With experience, we learned how to thwart their attacks and turn them to our advantage.

When the North African campaign ended in Tunisia in May 1943, I was a F/Lt. and had been a flight commander for eight months. I had flown 195 operational sorties, and my score in the air was 13 Me 109s, 1 Macchi 202, and 1 six-engined transport, plus many probables and damaged enemy fighters; while dive-bombing and ground strafing I claimed 8 enemy aircraft and 200 motor vehicles.

After a tour as gunnery instructor at El Ballah, near Cairo, Egypt, I returned to ops with 417

Ace pilot "Stocky" Edwards in his Spitfire coded JF-E, TD 147, leading a take-off. — photo Alan Bayly

RCAF Squadron in December 1943, in Italy, flying beautiful Spitfire VIIIs. Two weeks later I became a flight commander on 92 RAF Squadron in the same 244 RAF Wing, and managed to shoot down four more enemy fighters.

In March 1943 I was given command of 274 RAF Spitfire Squadron, only to have the squadron repatriated three weeks later with two other old desert squadrons, to bolster the fighter forces for D-day, the invasion of Europe.

We formed a new Spitfire Wing at Hornchurch, and commenced flying operations May 14,1944, with a wing sweep over the Continent. Our wing operated from Detling, West Malling and Tangmere, taking part in D-day operations, flying sweeps and escorts.

In late August the wing converted to Tempest aircraft to chase V-1 flying bombs. Shortly afterwards I was taken off operations and sent back to Canada.

I returned to flying operations in March 1945, promoted to wing commander, and became wing leader of 127 RCAF Spitfire Wing at Eindhoven. I managed to damage a few more enemy aircraft before the war ended.

On August 9, 1945, 127 Wing took off for the last time, flying back to Dunsfold to be disbanded. The wing pilots were happy to return to England, but not at all keen to give up their Spitfires forever.

My desire to fly the Spitfire on ops was unsurpassed by anyone, and to reach the ultimate position of wing commander flying of an entire RCAF Spitfire wing was the height of a fighter pilot's career.

The Spitfire was a joy and fun to fly. It was a superb combat aircraft, and in the hands of an experienced pilot, it was unequalled.

JFE, November 4, 1997

Art Sager at the controls of BL 772, a 421 Squadron Mk V coded AU-S. — courtesy Art Sager

PREFACE

FROM ALL PARTS OF CANADA, young people came forth to serve their country in World War II. A lucky, but sizable number of them went into combat flying the immortal Spitfire. An inspired design, it became the sword which would defeat the enemy in every major battle to which it was committed. In many cases, the person in the cockpit firing the guns was a Canadian.

The stories that follow are all first-person accounts, unlike so many books that depend on the well-meaning attempts of historians. The intent here is to produce as little distortion as possible, to let the reader know what it was like to fly the best aircraft of its time. Many books try to describe what people did, but here it is told by the actual person involved, in their own words.

Following the success of my first book to follow this formula, came a vast amount of new material, thanks to the momentum of research and personal contacts with the pilots. I was very pleased to have the assistance and contribution of Steven Fochuk for this second book, with his limitless energy and enthusiasm for Canadian fighter pilots.

No attempt is made to glorify war, but it must not be considered wrong to remember what happened, and to laud those who risked all in the cause of freedom. The scars these veterans carry, physically and emotionally, are badges of courage in the face of all odds. The evil that consumed the world from 1939 to 1945 continues to touch all of us to this day, in the way that events have unfolded since those years.

Readers should be aware of just how unique and timely the interviews have been. Many veterans are reluctant to be considered heroes, and for many it was the first, and often last time that they would be so candid about their feelings and experiences. As time goes by and takes its toll, the opportunity to obtain these accounts becomes less likely.

Canadians are renowned for their humility, yet their contribution to the war effort, and the fight against tyranny in all forms, was of enormous importance in winning World War II. More than fifty years later, the memories of those involved in the battles remain scorched and indelible. Getting it on paper was not always easy from their point of view, but most were ready and willing to convey some of their thoughts and experiences for future generations to appreciate.

For this book, I have had access to countless scrapbooks and photo albums kept by the pilots, their personal logbooks, and advice. Most interviews took place in person, some over the phone, and some pilots were able to respond by letter. Official sources and photos have also been used, but it was the veterans themselves who provided the best information — information not found in any archive.

The artwork depicts a variety of the types and different versions of the Spitfire flown by our Canadian pilots. Ron Lowry again provided the majority of the colour work through his talent and knowledge of his subject. Many show the aircraft of Canadian ace pilots, but this is not the only yardstick of the ability of many of our pilots. The considerable number of enemy aircraft downed by Canadians in combat proves that they were second to none in air combat.

I would also like to thank Almont Baltzer, Paul Lewis, Jeff Robinson, Steve Sauvé, Dorothée Skalde, Wayne Scott, and many others, for their contribution to this book. Thanks also to Janet at the Central Negative Library, and to all of the fighter pilots.

THE BATTLE OF BRITAIN

A. K. "Skeets" Ogilvie, 609 Squadron

BEFORE THE WAR, they had in the RAF what they called a "short service commission." You signed up for four years and became an officer, then you were expected to serve six years in the reserve. I had my name in to join the RAF in the summer of 1939. The war clouds were getting very black, and the RAF realized that it would need a few more people.

They called me up on a Monday, I took a medical on Wednesday, and sailed to England on Friday, in August of 1939. They didn't lose any time! I was in the last group of eight to join the RAF this way — the group behind us went into the RCAF.

In 1940 I joined 609 Squadron, flying the immortal Spitfire. On the day our fellows ran into the Stukas I was on the ground as duty pilot, a flare gun in my hand, out on the runway. I don't think the squadron paid much attention to me, as they took off on both sides of me. They found the Stukas, which had become separated from their Me 109 escort because of cloud, and it became a real turkey shoot. I never got to see any Stukas on my flights, because the Germans gave up using them after the losses they took.

The Messerschmitt 109 was our main opponent. It seemed to be able to fly higher than we could because of its direct fuel injection. At 30,000 feet the Spitfire was wallowing, whereas the 109s were still sailing along. However at 17,000–20,000 feet, the altitude at which most combats took place, the Spitfire was the master.

A 609 Squadron Spitfire I during the Battle of Britain. — photo P. Scott

German pilot Oblt. Weckeiser force-landed this Messerschmitt 110C-2 in England on September 27, 1940, after attacks by RAF fighters during the Battle of Britain. Note the four victory bars on the rudder. — photo courtesy Steve Fokchuk

We could out-turn the Messerschmitts, and at lower altitudes they were heavier on the controls, and sometimes would crash if they could not pull out of a dive.

September 7, 1940, was my baptism of fire. I remember the two 109Es below me, like they were only a few yards away. I could see the pilots in their brown leather jackets and helmets. They were leaning over, looking at the Heinkels they were escorting. I came up sun from them — I could see their bright yellow noses painted right up to their cockpits, and could read the numbers on the fuselages. I was absolutely mesmerized by the sight, then came to, and started to fire at the first one.

But it was the second one I hit. He shuddered, glycol came streaming out, and he went down.

My Spitfire, N 3280, was now low on fuel, and I was far from my base back at Middle Wallop. I was just starting to select a field to land in when I saw an airfield, which turned out to be a naval air station. I was on a learning curve, but if you weren't lucky, then you may as well have stayed home!

The Messerschmitt 110 twin-engine fighter was another aircraft we tangled with. On September 27, 1940, we came across one of their defensive circles over the English Channel. The 110s seemed to be waiting for their bombers to come back from England to escort them home.

7

Our flight commander was away at the time, so P/O F.G. "Mick" Miller, who was an Australian, was leading. He was in X 4107, PR-F, my usual aircraft. Mick led the squadron into the circle. One of their number turned to meet him, and they were looking at each other for a split second. Then they hit head-on.

I was Mick's number two, about fifty yards behind. There was a big sheet of flame all over the sky, with a Spitfire wing that rolled up and floated over the black smoke, and I could see the white strings of a parachute blowing away.

I pulled straight up, so I wouldn't collide with the debris, enough to get into a stall, rolled over, and came right down and got on the tail of a 110. I let him have it, and he went straight down, crashing somewhere in Bournmouth. I saw another 110 do a slow dive. I turned over to have a go at him, but was told by one of the other pilots, "Leave him alone, he's mine!" The 110 pilot didn't do anything but glide down, as two of our Spitfires flew tight formation with him, until he went kerplunk into the Channel.

[Editor's note: Postwar research shows that the 110 that Miller collided with was a 110C-4, W.Nr. 3297, coded 3U x FT of 9/ZG 26, and crashed at Dole Ash Farm, Piddletrenthide. The pilot, Gefr. Jackstedt, was taken POW. The radio operator was killed.]

Previous page: Members of 609 Squadron play a game of cricket. Canadian Tom Rigler is second from left. — RCAF official photo

THE BATTLE OF BRITAIN

William "Yank" Nelson, 74 Squadron

On October 17, 1940, I was Red Two of the leading section of 74 Squadron, flying Spitfires, and detailed to intercept sixty "snappers" (enemy aircraft) reported over Maidstone.

We climbed rapidly, and at 26,000 feet saw some bursts from our anti-aircraft guns below, and turned towards them. Two Me 109s suddenly appeared by themselves across our bows. The squadron leader, "Sailor" Malan, DFC, immediately got on the tail of the leading 109, and I closed with the outside one.

They took no evasive action as we came out of the sun, and I fired a burst with slight deflection at 150 yards, down to point blank range. He immediately started a half-roll turn down, white smoke streaming out, obviously glycol.

I followed him easily at first, firing short bursts, and then more eruptions came from his engine, almost blinding me. Diving down to 2,000 feet, he entered some low cloud vertically. Having got up tremendous speed, I had to start to pull out in order to avoid hitting the ground. I found him difficult to hold in the latter part of the dive, as he went well past vertical, and I had my actuating gear wound fully forward.

He was seen to crash near Gravesend. The enemy aircraft was coloured dark on top, with a tremendous yellow spinner, and was sky blue beneath.

[Editor's note: William Nelson, DFC and Bar, from Westmount, Quebec, achieved six victories in the Battle of Britain, but was killed during the battle, not long after this account was given. He was nicknamed "Yank" in the squadron, due to his Canadian accent.]

THE BATTLE OF BRITAIN

J. Stewart "Stew" Young , CD 234 Squadron

THE NEED FOR FIGHTER PILOTS in the late summer of 1940 was extreme. I had long had the flying bug, and had attained that wonder of wonders, my first solo, back in Edmonton, Alberta, on August 10, 1935. Then I put in lots of solo time while waiting for my licence. I saw in an advertisement that able young men were invited to fly for the RAF. It was the opportunity of a lifetime.

I became Acting Pilot Officer No. 39362, and fitted out with a uniform and a bank account, followed by tedious square bashing and other ground training, with some flying training to follow at Ternhill. At last I received the coveted pilot's wings, with an "above the average" rating in my logbook. I was posted to a bomber squadron to fly the ungainly, large (to us then), Armstrong Whitworth Whitley, Mark I.

I was thoroughly trained to fly bombing missions over Germany. I had well over 400 hours logged, and Britain had invested time and money in training me for the job. I was rather surprised to be sent to No. 2 Ferry Pilot's Pool, RAF Station Filton, but I received valuable experience flying a wide variety of aircraft — eighteen different types in a little over two months. The planes were as varied as D. H. Rapides and Blenheims, Wellingtons and Spitfires.

The early Spitfires had manual undercarriage controls; the throttle was on the right, and the undercarriage pump on the left — an awkward arrangement, as one pumped up the undercart after take-off, operating the throttle and the control column at the same time. The Spitfire was also difficult to taxi, for the long nose rose at a sharp angle when on the ground, and one had to weave from side to side to ensure that all was clear ahead. Once in the air, however, she flew with grace, speed, and beauty, and became my favourite aircraft by far.

November 1939 found me back labouring away in the ponderous Whitley Is again, at No. 7 Bombing and Gunnery School at Newton Down,

J. Stewart Young, C.D., 234 Squadron pilot who saw action during the Battle of Britain.

in South Wales. Throughout my service career, I often received postings that I would not have chosen. But I tried not to feel any disappointment, and as I had been caught up in the excitement of flying from an early age, it seemed that as long as I was flying, even the lumbering but stately old Whitley, I felt happy.

However, you can imagine my elation when my CO, Ira Jones, a distinguished World War I pilot, called me into his office and simply asked, "How would you like to be a fighter pilot?"

"Sure," I replied without hesitation.

"Well, we've been losing a lot of chaps," he said. "You might as well go and be a hero."

There was no time to waste on a lengthy training course, so I spent a total of eleven days at a Spitfire OTU course at Hawarden, doing formation flying, aerobatics, dogfighting practice, beam attacks, and battle patrols. September 19, 1940, found me reporting to 234 Fighter Squadron, at St. Eval, Cornwall.

It was no small honour to join the ranks of such seasoned and successful pilots. This squadron had just achieved the highest score in a single engagement by any squadron in the battle, on September 4. Attacking a formation of one hundred enemy aircraft, the squadron shot down fourteen Messerschmitt 110s and Dornier 17s, damaging several more, without any losses themselves. The pace had, however, taken its toll, and on one day, nine out of twelve of their aircraft had been lost. So the squadron moved to a relatively quiet area at St. Eval, in 10 Group, when I joined them.

While my logbook rated me as above the average in flying the Whitley, I was pleased to get much better at flying the Spitfire, thanks to Jan Zurakowski, one of the most skillful pilots I ever knew. Jan was one of two Polish pilots on the squadron while I was with them, and he gave me a lot of formation flying and dogfighting practice. Jan later became famous as the test pilot for the Avro Arrow in Canada, an aircraft that although years ahead of its time, was scrapped by the Diefenbaker government in 1959.

A lot of our flying was on patrols, protecting shipping, and seeking out and chasing off attacking Luftwaffe bombers. We were also tasked with protecting the busy harbours of Falmouth and Plymouth.

One day the pilots were sprawling in the dispersal hut, reading, waiting for whatever flying duty might crop up. I looked up, and spotted something red coming through the peak of the roof. We all realized that we were subject to another surprise attack from the Luftwaffe, with incendiaries pouring down on us. We dashed out of the hut, and just as we did so, one of the hangars burst into flames, and a petrol bowser received a direct hit. It literally took off, rising into the air as it broke into fragments. An Anson in one of the hangars also started to burn, and machine gun ammunition that was stored there went off as well, making it a volatile place to be.

On the evening of October 9, the Jerries brought the action right to our doorstep again. We were a day squadron in our Spitfires, with no night-flying facilities, and were about to call it a day, when we were attacked by Dornier 17s. Dusk was falling, and in addition, the sky was laden with dark, heavy rain clouds.

Consequently, it was virtually impossible to make out the dark-coloured Dorniers — I think there were only three or four of them. One of our pilots, Sgt. Bell, succeeded in shooting down one of the raiders, which was confirmed the next morning in Newquay Bay, near St. Mawgan.

We still had the job of returning to our airfield, which had no flare path. The only light available came from two sources — from the corner of one of the hangars, which a German bomb had set alight, and from streams of light that were streaking into the sky. It did not take me long to realize that these were tracer bullets coming in our direction, fired by our own Bofors anti-aircraft guns. Fortunately they missed us, just as they had missed the Dorniers. As I came in to the field on my approach, I reached up to switch on my navigation lights, thinking that at least they would make me visible enough for the other Spitfires to stay out of my way. I didn't realize until I was down that I had turned on the Pitot heater switch instead of the lights!

By great good fortune, we all got down that night without damage, except for Sgt. Bell, who had shot down the Dornier. He landed about fifteen feet too high and drove his undercarriage struts right through the wings when he did contact the deck. We just couldn't see to land well in the dark.

Hungry, we went to the mess, hoping for a meal. But everything was closed down; the staff were in the air raid shelters, and did not get our meal until the "all clear" had sounded.

Overleaf: "Whiskey," 401 Squadron mascot, in the cockpit of J.K. Ferguson's Mk IX Spitfire, YO-F, BR 159, August 1942. — photo Fiander

THE FIRST FW 190

Omer Levesque, 401 Squadron

Omer Levesque in the cockpit of YO-V, AA 973. His usual Spitfire was YO-Q, for Quebec, with that province's coat of arms painted on the folding door. — courtesy Omer Levesque

AT THE END OF THE SUMMER OF 1941, we did quite a few sweeps. We had been up north in 12 Group, but now we were in 11 Group, at Biggin Hill.

On November 22, 1941, we didn't expect to see any Focke-Wulf 190s. We mostly saw 109s, the standard Luftwaffe fighter up to that time. So when the Focke-Wulfs appeared, they took us by surprise.

My flight commander was Hank Sprague, a veteran of the Battle of Britain, and a very experienced pilot. I was right behind him. We had just made a turn over Boulogne as we were coming back. I looked to my left for just a split second, and Hank was gone. I just saw a parachute floating — that's how fast it happened. (Hank in AD 516)

Well, the Focke-Wulf 190 that just got him wound up right in front of me. The sky was clear blue, and I could see the radial engine as he twisted and turned, and underneath the plane was a light bird's egg blue. From the side, I could see some yellow colour on the spinner, and the top of the cowl of the engine was also yellow. It was not at all like a 109, with its in-line engine. The canopy was very modern looking, and I could see the pilot from his elbow and upper chest in profile as he was turning — as I fired at him.

I probably took him by surprise, and white smoke came out from the fuselage. Then he pulled right in front of me again, and down in a dive. I followed him down, making turns and climbing back up, continuing to make shots. After what seemed like half an hour, but was in reality only three to five minutes perhaps, he made another dive. I followed him, firing 20 mm shells and machine guns. It was a very long, steep dive — we were both going well over 400 mph — which really made the Spit I was in stiff on the controls. I was using tail trimming and elevator tabs to control the aircraft, and was starting to throttle back when we were down to 2,000 feet. I pulled out of the dive, but the Focke-Wulf 190 didn't.

When I was climbing back up, I spotted some more enemy aircraft that seemed to be a mix of 109s and 190s. I fired at another FW 190, but even though I could see some hits, because of the wild dogfight I was not sure of the result. So I only claimed a damaged or probable for the second one.

The Focke-Wulf I had downed was one of the first reported, if not the first shot down, although some Blenheim aircraft had seen them a few days before. We had received very little notice — we thought they might have been captured Curtiss 75s that the French had been using, and the Germans had put a spinner on them. I made my report to the intelligence officer, and made my sketch. The tail looked a bit like a Stuka, and the rest of the wing and engine reminded me of a Harvard, but much more powerful, and with a spinner. My sketch was a pretty good likeness, if I say so, and very soon we saw a lot more of the Focke-Wulfs in combat.

As for the Spitfire that I had flown that day (W 3178, YO-Q), a Mark V, it never flew right after that, and was found to have suffered some popped rivets and structural damage from my wild fight. It was taken away to be repaired or scrapped.

"Hank" Sprague with his Spitfire V, "Harriet," YO-P, AD 451, in November 1941. — RCAF official photo PMR-78-95

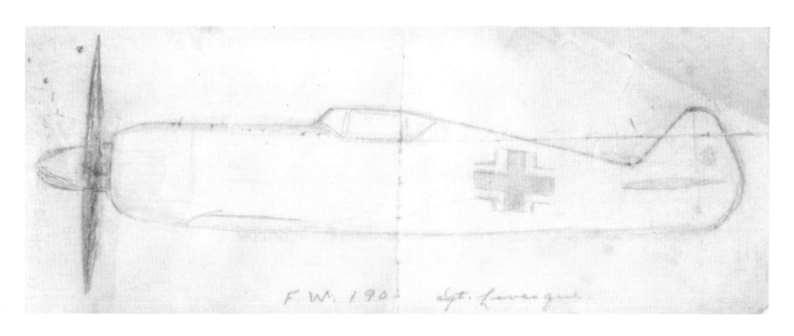

Omer Levesque's sketch for the intelligence officer of the new German FW190 compared well with the photograph of the real thing. —courtesy Omer Levesque

JERSEY I

Ian "Ormy" Ormston

I FLEW IN 401 SQUADRON, RCAF. The photo shows Sgt. Lyon Kay standing on the wing root preparing to help a young pilot officer, Ian Campbell Ormston ("Ormy" for short), into the cockpit. We were both from Montreal, old pals from West Hill High School.

Anyway, the picture shows my aircraft, YO-E, a Mark V, serial number AA 926, which I flew from November 1, 1941, onwards. It was a special aircraft, being a presentation aircraft. I personally accepted the cheque for $25,000 from W. A. Black, another Montrealer, and a delightful old Victorian-style gentleman (I still remember the old-fashioned collar he wore).

He had my Spitfire named *Jersey I* after the English Channel Island to which he retired after relinquishing the presidency of Ogilvie Flour Mills, although he had to leave the island when the Nazis took it over. My Spitfire was one of two (*Jersey I* and *Jersey II*) that he donated. There was also a maple leaf for Canada painted on the aircraft [an early application of this motif — ed.], and on the other side, my future wife's name, Marguerite, was painted on the nose. She and I had been going out since 1939, and she is still my wife today (1997).

Mr. Black's investment started to pay off right away. On November 22, 1941, I was able to claim a 109E destroyed. I remember we were flying at 15,000 feet when I dove down to attack the 109s below us at 8,000 feet. I saw a 109 flying straight ahead of me in a gentle dive, and I followed, firing, but with no visible results. Then I broke off to attack a 109 above me doing a left-hand turn. In banking, he presented a full plan view, and I started firing my remaining ammo.

He dove vertically, and I followed, seeing him crash in a field 10 miles south of Marck.

On another flight in YO-E, on February 12, 1942, we were eight miles off Calais, at only 1,000 feet, when we spotted two 109s ahead of us. They began to climb, and we gave chase. I got into a good line

astern position, got close in, and fired. Flames shot out, and he went into a dive and crashed.

Climbing, the other 109 sailed across right in front of us, and three of us fired at him, and Al Harley followed him until he also crashed.

I flew that aircraft almost constantly until May 1942, when I received another. We were part of the Bigin Hill Wing and remained constantly in action against the Luftwaffe, with their 109s and 190s.

P/O Ian Ormston is helped into the cockpit of his Spitfire V, YO-E, AA 926, by Sgt. Lyon Kay on February 12, 1942. The aircraft, one of the first to be marked with a maple leaf below the windscreen, was donated to the RCAF by W.A. Black, a Montreal businessman and the president of Ogilvie Flour Mills. Black had retired to the island of Jersey, but left when the island was abandoned to the Nazis. His gift of the Spitfire Jersey I was his revenge. The aircraft carried Ormston's wife's name, Marguerite, on the port side. — RCAF official photo PL 7049

DIEPPE COMBAT

T. Ibbotson, 401 Squadron

ON AUGUST 19, 1942, I was flying Spitfire IX (BS 104, YO-R, with the nose art shown in the photo), in 401 Squadron. Over Dieppe, I saw an FW 190 positioned above, at four o'clock to me. I broke to port, closing to 150 yards, and opened fire on the enemy aircraft, using thirty degrees of deflection. I observed strikes all along the cockpit and towards the rear of the fuselage.

The FW 190 flicked on his back, and I gave him another burst from above, and saw strikes on the belly. He went into a spin, to about 13,000 feet. I followed him down, and fired another short burst, but observed no further hits.

The Focke-Wulf continued to spin to about 7,000 feet, then went down in a dive, with every appearance that the pilot had been killed.

This enemy aircraft was claimed as probably destroyed.

F/O T.K. Ibbotson flew Spitfire YO-R, BS 104, at Dieppe. It explodes the myth that only the Yanks had nose art on their aircraft.

Howard Simpson driving, with Free French pilot René Foukes as passenger. — courtesy Ian Keltie

RODEO 115

Howard A. Simpson, 402 Squadron

Yes, THAT'S ME ON THE MOTORCYCLE, which I purchased for seven pounds. René Foukes (Free French) is behind me. In the background is S/Lt. "Bud" Malloy's Spitfire IX, BS 430. We were based at Kenley, just outside of London.

My most memorable day has to be December 4, 1942. The wing commander had organized a fighter escort to some American bombers into France. So we went across the Channel, flying up and up. I was flying on the portside in Spitfire IX BS 309, AE-G, although my usual aircraft was AE-Q (*Queenie*).

What happened was we got into a gaggle of enemy fighters — FW 190s. The last thing I heard was, "Break port" from S/Lt. Malloy, so I threw my aircraft into a steep turn to the left, with stick back. I passed out, owing to the G-force (it also appears that my oxygen system was not working).

The boys later said that they saw me go down, level off, come up, and fall off again. Finally I came to. I was at 14,000 feet, surrounded by six Focke-Wulfs — two up in front, and two each to the sides. One of them in front of me fired a burst, and I saw a couple of holes appear in my wings. I had to do something — fast.

I hawked her into a turn, pulled the stick back, and I was on the tail of that FW 190. I proceeded to shoot his tail off. Looking back, I saw some FW 190s behind me, so I tightened my turn and broke towards them. I straightened up slightly, and saw an FW 190 in front of me. I was right behind him, and fired several more bursts. The 190 rolled slowly over on his back to the left, with me following him. I got to within 200 yards and saw a flash on his fuselage between the cockpit and tailplane.

He dove away, and I followed him, firing for a while until I had used up all of my ammo.

I then thought to myself, "Simpson, you better get the hell out of there!" so I rolled over on my back, and went down at full throttle. The Spitfire was going so fast that the wings were bending, and I thought they were going to come off. I was doing well over 500 mph.

It was a very hazy day, and I thought I had better level off before I hit the water, so I throttled back and came out right over the water near St. Emer. The main thing was, the FW 190s were gone.

It was not the best place to be — that low — so I climbed back up to 20,000 feet to see where I was. I could see France on one side, and England over on the other. I was just getting my bearings when my engine seized up: the four blades just stopped like that. What a feeling! Now what am I gonna do?

I managed to glide all the way back across the Channel and landed on the beach at Dungerness. It was wheels-up, right on the shale, dead-stick, but one of my better landings actually. (My windscreen was also all oiled up, so it was so hard to see.)

I got out and ran a short distance, because there was smoke billowing out and I thought it might blow up. Along comes a car down a road on the hill. It was the commanding officer of a tank regiment based at Lydd. He had a fire extinguisher, so he and I ran back to the Spit and started squirting it, and stopped it from burning.

I checked to see the guns were unloaded, and found only one 303 round left in the clip, which I kept as a souvenir for many years. They gave me a triple shot of scotch because they thought I needed it, and I slept most of the way back to my unit!

Baptism of Fire

Lawrence "Doc" Somers, 403 Squadron

I WAS A MEMBER OF 403 SQUADRON. After several operational fights, on March 24, 1942, in my first real contact with the enemy, I managed to shoot down an FW 190. I was flying my usual Spitfire, BL 707, KH-Y. I fired a burst of my cannons, and the enemy plane plunged to earth, with smoke pouring from its fuselage. I didn't have time to be too elated, as I was then attacked by another, and gave him a squirt with my machine guns. I might have caused him some damage. When I landed, a photo was taken of the nineteen-year-old kid who did the deed, and the caption used in the newspapers said that it was my "baptism of fire." It was to be a prophetic statement.

We continued our sweeps, and I recall being made B Flight commander when the usual fellow went on leave. I felt quite proud of this position, because they went over the heads of two pilot officers quite senior to me.

June 2, 1942, is a day I will not forget. Our formation ran into thirty of the FW 190s. Just the day before, one had put a hole three feet by five feet in my left wing. This time, a burst from an enemy fighter hit my aircraft, causing gasoline to seep into the cockpit. We finally managed to elude the Focke-Wulfs, and, out of ammunition, were on our way home when we were attacked by another thirty or so of the new German fighters.

We were at 30,000 feet, and a blast from an FW 190 turned my cockpit into a blazing inferno. I was blinded by the smoke and flames, and hardly knew what I was doing. I remember pulling the ring to release my parachute, but I knew I had done the wrong thing, as I was not clear of the aircraft. I then pulled the pin which released the harness that fastened me in the cockpit, and then I guess I must have lost consciousness.

The next thing I remember was a terrific swish, and a jerk, and I realized that in some manner I had fallen clear of the plane. How I ever got clear with my parachute already released in the cockpit, I never will know.

The next thing I noticed was that all of my clothes, my oxygen mask, and most of my Mae West had been burned off me. All that was left of my clothing were my shoes and socks and little bits of cloth under the parachute harness, which were still smouldering. I finally got them out and then unfastened the rubber dinghy from the seat in the parachute harness. Luckily, the pack was fireproof, and the dinghy was not damaged.

My hands and arms were so badly burned that I could not operate the release on my parachute harness, and when I hit the water I was buried in shrouds and silk. As I went under the water, I turned the valve which released the gas from the bottle attached to the dinghy. As the dinghy filled with gas, I gradually came to the surface, and although I could breathe, I was still buried in the parachute. I worked steadily for half an hour before I got the chute clear of the dinghy, and by this time I was sick because I had swallowed a considerable amount of water.

I hardly remember anything of those two days I spent on the water. My eyes swelled shut, and I was too badly burned to try to paddle. Part of the time I slept, and part of the time I was unconscious. I was without food or water. I didn't even hear the motor boat that approached me on the second day until it was right alongside of me. I didn't know where I was, and I couldn't see, so I didn't know it was a German boat until someone spoke to me.

I was lifted into the boat, and immediately two nurses started to treat my burns. Neither of them could speak English, but I could speak some German, which I had learned in school, and I was able to ask for a drink.

When we landed I was treated by German doctors, first at Boulogne, and then at St. Omer Hospital. In the second hospital I received lousy treatment. For five days I was left in a room without having any of my dressings changed, as I had refused to give them any information about my unit except my name and number. Finally, when they found out I would not talk, I was moved to another prison camp hospital which was staffed by British doctors.

The British doctors found I had also received a bullet through the top of my left ear. At Stradtroda, I was eventually feeling well enough to assist in taking care of other prisoners, including Canadians who had been wounded at Dieppe.

I was moved around to various prison camps, and when the Russians commenced their advance from the east, we were forced to go on the march in January. We walked as far as 20 miles in a day, in 30 below zero weather, and a lot of the men suffered frostbite. Fortunately, we were issued Red Cross parcels before we started, or we would have starved. In fact, if it had not been for the Red Cross, we would have starved no matter where we were in prison camps.

After walking 150 miles, and then travelling another three days by truck, the Allies came in from the west, and we were forced to march another 200 miles back again. It was grim, but I got home even though there were many times when I never thought I would. It was a miracle that I came out of it alive, and I can't begin to tell you what it meant for me to get home.

Lawrence "Doc" Somers with his Spitfire V, KH-Y, BL 707, on March 24, 1942. — RCAF official photo PL 7419

First World War ace Billy Bishop visits RCAF 402 Squadron in 1942. S/L Norm Bretz stands second left, with hands together. — RAF photo 18428 courtesy Ian Keltie

Harlen "Bub" Fuller goes hunting for the Hun with a shotgun and Spitfire V, AE-H, BM 509. — courtesy Ian Keltie

LIFEBOAT SEARCH

Art Sager, 421 Squadron

THAT PHOTO OF ME PROBABLY SHOWS AU-E, as that was my usual aircraft when the photo was taken in the spring of 1943. Our first adjutant, Charles Chasanoff, was the man who got the Indian crest for 421 from McColl-Frontenac, (it was their emblem), and we were the "Red Indian" Squadron.

On January 2, 1943, I was flying BL 339, AU-F, on a lifeboat search. A convoy had been attacked in the English Channel on New Year's Day. Several ships had been damaged, and two sunk. While B Flight remained on readiness, A Flight was sent in sections of two, to search for survivors.

When my number two, Fleming, and I reached our assignment area, we started a north-south search at 5,000 feet. The recent storm had abated, but seas were still high with white-caps, and it was cold. Fortunately, the cloud base was at 7,000 feet, and visibility was good. Near the end of the first leg, we saw a small coastal freighter steaming south. We flew west one minute, and then north, wide apart, weaving and tipping the wings to look below.

Suddenly I saw, or thought I could, a spot on the sea that was more than a crashing wave. Signalling Fleming, I dove down. At 1,000 feet, the spot became a boat. At 500 feet, an open lifeboat. And at 50 feet I saw two men, one lying motionless in the middle, the other slouched at the stern, looking up. He raised his arm slowly, as if it were an effort to do so. I waggled my wings to show I had seen him.

I climbed back up to 5,000 feet, circling to keep the lifeboat in view, and called ops to report that we were going to try to divert a nearby ship to the rescue. Fleming remained circling to give ops a fix, and I went full throttle on a guess-estimate course for the freighter. When I saw it, I dropped down slowly to 300 feet and flew starboard on a parallel course to identify myself. Then, down at 50 feet, I went around the ship, wagging my wings.

There were two men on the bridge, one with binoculars. I flew ahead of the ship, turned and went back on a reciprocal course in the direction of the lifeboat. Going as slowly as I could on the port side of the ship, I waved my hands forward, hoping the man with the binoculars would see my signal. I continued flying north, tipping my wings.

I was not sure they understood, so I repeated the manoeuvre a second time, pulling back the hood and pointing, my open hand going back and forth. Still, there was no reaction.

On the third try, I pressed the gun button for five seconds after passing the ship, and the bullets sprayed the water. If that didn't get the attention of the captain, nothing would! It did the trick, and when I went back for a fourth try, the ship had stopped. Then it turned quickly, and reversed its course.

I wagged my wings with joy, and started to lead

Opposite: Art Sager in the cockpit of a 421 Squadron Spitfire V. — RCAF official photo PL 19035

In this May 1943 photograph, 421 Squadron can be seen gathered around S/L J.D. Hall's Spitfire V, AU-A, BM 316, nicknamed "Smokeater III." Note the unusual camouflage paint job. — RCAF official photo PL 19043

the way, back and forth like a whippet leading a tortoise. I called Fleming and told him the ship was coming, and he told control. Finally, after a long thirty minutes, Fleming called to say he could see me as well as the ship, ploughing the seas behind.

We circled the lifeboat until the freighter was within a hundred yards, and then, worrying about petrol, we climbed back up to 5,000 feet and returned to base. We never learned whether the men in the lifeboat were picked up alive, but we did feel happy to have found the lifeboat. I felt sure that at least the man who waved at us must have been OK.

HEADING NOT CLEAR

Doug "Duke" Warren, 165 Squardron

THE SOUTHEAST PORTION OF ENGLAND was covered by 11 Group Fighter Command. This was the area where most fighter operations took place at this time, and corresponded roughly to the area where the Battle of Britain had been fought two years before. In effect we were going into battle.

One night Duke and I had a serious talk about the future and what it might bring. We knew casualties occurred among fighter pilots everywhere, but were far more likely to occur in the south, where air to air fighting took place. We recognized that one or both of us might be injured in a crash, wounded, or killed. And the intelligence reports indicated that this was more than likely — at least a 50-50 chance.

We were not distressed by our conversation, and indeed our main concern was the likely reaction of our parents, or of any parent who lost a son or daughter. We were aware that our parents were against our joining up because of the potential danger. Even before leaving Canada we had witnessed the reaction of parents and families who had lost a member due to a flying accident or other tragic event. But we had a Christian belief that everything was in the hands of the Lord, and he would make the decisions.

We did agree on one thing. We cautioned each

The Warren twins of 165 Squadron RAF. Left is Duke I (Bruce) and at right Duke II (Doug). — courtesy Duke Warren

F/O R.C. "Scotty" McRoberts shortly after shooting down two Me 109s on July 5, 1944, with his Spitfire, AU-S, MJ 569.

— RCAF official photo PL30719

Douglas "Duke" Warren's Spitfire V when he was in 165 Squadron RAF. — courtesy Duke Warren

other not to go crazy and go against impossible odds in a fit of rage if one should see the other get shot down, or crash. Looking back now perhaps we were being overconfident in our ability to maintain self-control under those circumstances, but we were lucky, and were never put to the test.

In August 1942 the squadron flew south to join 11 Group. Our destination was Gravesend on the Thames, east of London. We were to be part of the famous Biggin Hill Wing. We landed at Woodvale to refuel, and I was delayed there because of an engine problem. On the 16th I left for Gravesend, and shortly after takeoff I saw two Spitfires collide in the air. Both crashed and there were no parachutes, so I landed at Hawarden (where I had suspected the aircraft had come from) and reported the accident and location of the crash. When I arrived at Gravesend I found the squadron had moved to Eastchurch. A further twenty-minute flight and I was at Eastchurch, where Duke already had a room organized for us in the mess.

The 165 Squadron was a new squadron that had not operated in the south before, and further training was considered necessary. We did two training flights, and a sweep towards Le Touget, with the Biggin wing leader leading the formation. These took place on the 17th, with another training flight on the 18th.

On the evening of the 18th a special briefing was held for all the wing pilots. This was rather a surprise for most pilots, including the senior leaders, for we were told that a large combined operation was to take place the next day. Furthermore, because the briefing took place after dinner, the ships carrying a large contingent of Canadian soldiers were already bound for the target, Dieppe. This was very exciting news, and it was pointed out that no phone calls were to be made, and personnel were not to leave the station.

Following the main briefing, our squadron commander briefed the pilots. It was to be a maximum effort, and takeoff would be at first light, before the sun would be up. Duke and I were to fly together in one of the first sections to take off. So off we went to our room to get some sleep before the early morning call.

Naturally we were very excited about the raid, and about the fact that the Canadian Army would be in the forefront, for we had many friends who had enlisted in various regiments. We had been told it was only a "raid in force" and there was no intention of staying. There was a small airstrip just outside Dieppe, and we were instructed that if we had to force land there, and did so before 11:00 A.M., the Canadian Army would take us back to the United Kingdom with them. But only up until 11:00 A.M. After that the army would have left for their return to the landing craft. Another important piece of information was that the Royal Navy had carte blanche to shoot at any aircraft below 7,000 feet, so we were to stay above that height over the ships.

Wakened very early, we took off just as the sun was coming up and proceeded to Dieppe. Patrolling at about 18,000 feet we could see the flashes of gunfire below us, and the landing craft near the beach. Of course our flying took most of our attention, and one only caught brief glimpses of the battle. During this first sortie we saw a good number of Spitfires, but neither we nor any other squadron saw enemy aircraft. Returning to Eastchurch via Beachy Head we landed after an hour and forty minutes of flying. Immediately the ground crew refuelled the aircraft and we were placed on readiness.

The second sortie was a far different story, for by this time the Luftwaffe had taken to the air with both fighters and bombers. There was an attack by Dornier 217 bombers which our squadron engaged. One bomber was shot down by our Yellow Section — F/Lt. Colquhoun, P/O Pederson (an American in the RAF), Duke as number three and me as number four. The crew bailed out and the bomber crashed into the sea.

This sortie lasted an hour and forty-five minutes, and we were all very short on fuel when we landed. Several aircraft ran out of fuel as the nose came up on landing, and they rolled to the end of the runway and turned off.

The third sortie took place in the afternoon. The troops had started their withdrawal some time before, and we were told there were no more Canadians on the beach, but what they really meant was that there were no more Canadians fighting. They were prisoners if they were alive. There were also many dead and wounded. However, we did patrol over the returning boats, and watched a destroyer, in mid-channel, burn and sink. Since we had never seen a large ship on fire we were amazed by how well a steel ship appeared to burn.

The squadron did a fourth sortie, but Duke and I were not on it. It had no contact with the Luftwaffe, chiefly covering the withdrawal of the boats which, by the time of the sortie, were close to the English coast. The squadron's final score for the day was two DO 217 destroyed, and four damaged, with no loss to ourselves.

Pilots taking part in the combined operation on August 19 knew it was a "big show," as such episodes were described then. Only later did we learn how big it was, for the RAF had flown almost 3,000 sorties, the Luftwaffe 945. At the time, it was thought losses were about equal, 100 aircraft on each side, but it was later found the Germans had only lost 50, whereas the Allies lost 106.

Dieppe, over the years, has become a very controversial subject for the historians. They all have theories, but most agree that, as terrible as the Canadian casualties were, the lessons learned saved many thousands of lives on D-day two years later.

Lorne Cameron, DFC, atop his personal Spitfire IX, AE-W, BS 152, in 402 Squadron RCAF, 1942. — courtesy Steve Sauvé

A Long Time Ago

Lorne M. Cameron, 402 Squadron

It has been fifty-six years since AC-2, L. M. Cameron R86269 became a lowly member of His Majesty's RCAF on January 2, 1941. At times it feels more like a hundred!

Anyway, I can tell you that the picture of me taking it easy on Spitfire IX, BS 152, AE-W, shows the aircraft I flew the most at the time the picture was taken. I checked my logbook, and it was taken in early 1943, at Kenley Airport, just south of London. One of my ground crew was the artist.

On February 27, 1943, I was flying as Blue Three in that aircraft, north of Dunkirk over the Channel, when four FW 190s followed us out, with more behind them. They started to close behind us, so the CO gave the order to break. F/O Norm Keene and I broke to port into the outermost of the four enemy aircraft. We pulled straight up

into him, and he turned to starboard, leaving us right on his tail.

I closed to one hundred yards, and fired. I could see strikes all along the port side of his fuselage, and he slowly turned over and dived away. I saw a splash in the water a few seconds after I had finished firing, and proceeded back to base.

The 402 Squadron was soon afterwards transferred off operations to RAF Station Digby, Lincolnshire, on March 22, 1943, for a so-called rest in 12 Group. Several of us who had completed a tour of operations were transferred to operational training units as instructors for six months. Then, we were posted to fighter squadrons in 11 Group. I went to Biggin Hill, to 401 Squadron just outside London, where I completed a second tour after D-day in June 1944.

Lorne Cameron's Spitfire IX, AE-W, BS 152, in 1942. One for the modellers! — courtesy Steve Sauvé

A HOT DAY

Ian Keltie, 402 and 442 Squadrons

AUGUST 24, 1942, was a particularly hot day, as I recall. It was to be a hot day in more ways than one.

We were escorting a bunch of American bombers in the daylight, coming back from deep in France. We were over, or near Boulogne, when we were bounced by fifty FW 190s. There were twelve of us. We got into a dogfight, and I was busy shooting at an FW 190, when there was a big bang in my Spitfire. I looked around, and I was under attack. The cockpit cover flew off, and at the same moment I felt something hit me in the leg, just like someone hit you with a hammer.

I took violent evasive action, and climbed as hard and fast as possible to get rid of the FW 190 that was so close to me. I tried not to turn my head too much at that point, as I didn't want to lose the new sunglasses I was wearing. It seemed important at the time!

When I was sure I was alone, I figured it was time for me to start going back to England, so I pushed the nose down. My leg just felt numb, so I was not in too much pain. I was halfway back across the Channel when I spotted two aircraft flying towards England. As I ran up closer, I found that they were two more FW 190s. This time I caught them by surprise. I opened fire on the second one trailing behind the first, and immediately saw black smoke coming from him, as he went down. There was no way I could stick around to see what happened, as the number one FW 190

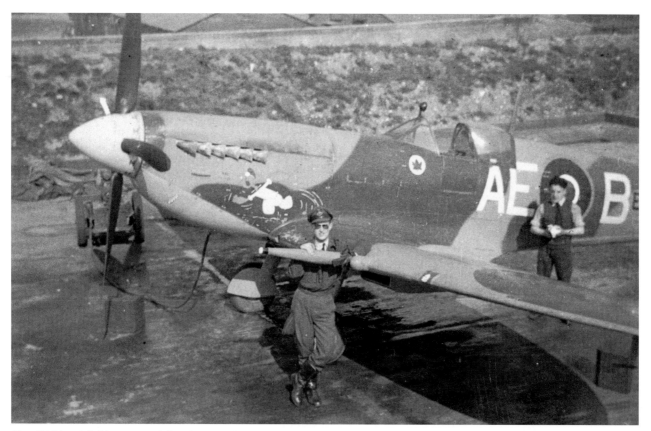

Ian Keltie with his personal Spitfire IX, "Popeye," AE-B, EN 398, in March 1943. In February it had been coded AE-I. Soon after, it became the most famous Spitfire of all, coded JE-J, the mount of W/C J.E. "Johnnie" Johnson.

— courtesy Ian Keltie

Ian Keltie, one of the few surviving Canadians to have flown a Spitfire in World War II, died last week at 86. He is shown in a 1943 photo.

DEATHS

CREWSON, Rhoda — Peacefully at Headwaters Health Care Centre, Orangeville on Friday, February 2, 2007 in her 86th year. Loving wife of the late Bill Crewson. Devoted mother of Edward and his wife Wendy. Cherished grandmother of Jennifer, Brooke and William. Predeceased by her sisters Ruby and Bessie and her infant sister Olive. The family will receive friends at the Doney Funeral Home, 318 Main St. E., Shelburne on Sunday from 7-9 p.m. and on Monday from 7-9 p.m. The funeral service will be held at Trinity United Church, Shelburne on Tuesday, February 6, 2007 at 2:00 p.m. Interment at Shelburne Cemetery. If desired, donations to the charity of your choice would be appreciated.

DaSILVA JARDINE, Joseph Ignace — Peacefully after a brief illness on Saturday, February 3, 2007 at North York General Hospital, 85 years. Beloved husband of Jean Luis (nee Nunes). Loving step-father of step-daughters. Beloved uncle of many nieces, nephews and great-nieces and nephews. Loving brother of Claude, Julio and Anthony. Loving brother-in-law of Ann and Irma. Predeceased by sisters Daphne and Muriel, brothers Ben and Cephas, sister-in-law Mary and brother-in-law David Camacho. Funeral Mass on Tuesday at 10 a.m. in Annunciation Church (Victoria Park, South of Ellesmere). Interment Mt. Hope Cemetery. In lieu of flowers, donations can be made in Ignace's memory to North York General Hospital. Arrangements entrusted to the Paul O'Connor Funeral Home.

DONALD, Jenny — Suddenly, as a result of an automobile accident, on Thursday, February 1, 2007, Jenny Donald, of London, at the age of 64. Wife of the late Fraser Boa (1992). Loving mother of Lee and her husband Rein Lomax and Greg and his wife Sandra, all of London. Cherished gran of Harrison and Erik. Dear daughter of Tichon and the late Sofie Borysewicz of Thunder Bay. Cremation has taken place. A memorial visitation will be held at WESTVIEW FUNERAL CHAPEL, 709 Wonderland Road North, London, on Wednesday from 7:00 - 9:00 p.m., where the Memorial Service will be conducted on Thursday, February 8, 2007 at 1:00 p.m. In lieu of donations, and in keeping with Jenny's love of flowers, please send flowers.

DOODCHENKO, Michael — With great sadness we announce the passing of Michael John Doodchenko, on Friday, February 2, 2007, at his home in Sandford, at the age of 51. Beloved husband to Sherry. Loving father to Amanda. Beloved son of Leo and Joan Doodchenko. Dear brother of Stephen and his wife Donna, and Kathy and her husband Nelson Cheung. Dear uncle of Taylor and Cameron Doodchenko, and Kayley Cheung. Fondly remembered by his in-laws Cliff and Dorothy Morris, Heather and Gord Balas, Mike Morris and ...

DEATHS

ALMERINDA CARVALHO FERREIRA (MACIEL)

Peacefully at Burton Manor, Brampton, on Sunday, February 4, 2007, at the age of 83 years, Almerinda, beloved wife of the late Albano Maciel. Loving mother of Albano (Isobel) of Azores, Portugal, Adriana Maciel (Lori) of Windsor, Ana (Emanuel Barbosa) of Brampton, Helena (Joe Correia) of Windsor, and Eduardo (Nelia) of Brampton, and of the late Jose Luis. Cherished "Avó" of Elizabeth, Laura, Mike, Tanya, Ashlee, Judy, Isaac, Bruno, Steven, Kevin, Luisinho, and Ricardo. Dear brother of Jacinto Ferreira. She will be greatly missed by many nieces, nephews and relatives. Special thanks to the nurses and staff at Burton Manor for all of their wonderful care and support. The family will receive friends at the Scott Funeral Home, 289 Main Street North "Brampton Chapel," 905-451-1100, on Tuesday, February 6, 2007 from 2 - 4 and 6 - 9 p.m. A Funeral Mass will be celebrated at Our Lady of Fatima Church in Brampton on Wednesday, February 7, 2007 at 10:00 a.m. Interment to follow at Brampton Memorial Gardens. Sign an online book of condolences at www.scott-brampton.ca

DEATHS

GRIGNON, Barbara (nee Tomlinson) — Passed away peacefully at North York General Hospital, surrounded by her husband and family on Friday, February 2, 2007, at the age of 85 years. Beloved wife of Philippe for 62 years. Loving mother of Paul (Tsiporah) Grignon and Margaret (Kevin) Squires. Cherished grandmother of Daniel, Shira, Tobias, Nicolette, Katherine, Jennifer, Stephanie, Laura and great-grandmother of Nikola, Hanna and Gabriel. Dear sister of Douglas Tomlinson and the late Marjorie Hedges. Barbara will also be missed by extended family of cousins, nieces and nephews in Canada and England. A private family inurnment service will be held at the Highland Memory Gardens Cemetery. Donations to your favourite charity would be appreciated by the family.

GRINTON, Georges – 1939 - 2007

From Chambly, on February 1, 2007, at the age of 67. He is survived by his sister Mina, his brothers Dave (Heather), Murray (Janet), his nieces Heather and Nicole, his nephews David (Lori), Kent, Michael (Lori), Andrew, Tyler, Luke, Dylan, his aunt Min Draper, his cousins Dianne Draper and many others, brother-in-law to Laura and Richard of Calgary, Alberta.

Viewing at La Maison Darche Dignity, 933 Périgny Blvd., Chambly, QC on Tuesday, February 6, 2007 from 2 p.m. to 5 p.m. and 7 p.m. to 9 p.m. Then at Jerrett Funeral Home, 660 Kennedy Rd., Scarborough, ON, on Thursday, February 8, 2007 from 2 p.m. to 4 p.m. and 7 p.m. to 9 p.m. Funeral will be held at the Chapel on Friday, February 9, 2007 at 11 a.m. Donations to Chiropractic Foundation of Quebec, 7950 Metropolitain Blvd. East, Ville D'Aniou, QC H1K' 1A1, telephone 514-352-0270, will be appreciated.

HAMILTON, Hazel (nee Graham) — We lost our mother, grandmother, friend and confidant on January 31, 2007, in her 85th year. She died with grace and honour, peacefully, surrounded by her loving family. Predeceased by Roy, her husband and best friend of 40 years, parents Hugh and Louisa Graham and brother Frank (Dorothy). Adored mother of Margaret, Jeanette (David) and Patricia (David). Treasured Nana of Sonya, Jocelyn and Ben. Cherished aunt to Bill (Chris) and step-grandmother to Holly and Heidi. She loved all of her friends and companions, especially at the United Church. While we have lost her physical presence, she lives within our hearts. We will always draw from the strength and compassion she showed to us all. Special thanks to Doctors Sidenberg and Aggarwal and the ICU nurses at William Osler Health Centre, Etobicoke. Family and friends will be received at the Ward Funeral Home, 2035 Weston Rd. (north of Lawrence Ave.), Weston on Monday and Tuesday from 7-9 p.m. A Memorial Service will be held at Martingrove United Church (75 Pergola Rd.) ...

DEATHS

JARVIS, Linda (Pollard) – 1950 - 2007

Linda passed on peacefully, at the Humber River Regional Hospital - Finch Site, on February 1, 2007. She has been released from the pain and struggle of a lengthy illness. Darling bride and sweetheart of Henry in their 39th year of marriage. Daughter of Lois and the late Henry Pollard. Loving mother of Kathleen (Jason), Kevin (Wendy), Chris, and Paul (Kirstan). She will be sadly missed by grandchildren Matthew, Megan, Tara, Joshua, Damonn, Emily and Bronwyn. Beloved sister of Patricia (Bram) and Ron (Jane). She was an aunt to 26 nieces and nephews. Linda's love of life, precious gifts of kindness and the manner in which she lived provides an extraordinary example of character for all. Family and friends may call at the Ward Funeral Home, 2035 Weston Road on Monday from 2-4 p.m and 7-9 p.m. Funeral Service in the Chapel on Tuesday at 1 p.m. Cremation to follow.

KEKEWICH, Olive Louisa, nee McNichol — Gone home to be with the Lord. At Toronto General Hospital on Friday, February 2, 2007 in her 97th year; beloved wife of the late Clarence Edward Kekewich; dear sister of Marion Bryant; also sadly missed by her other relatives and many friends; predeceased by her sisters Jean McNichol, Frances Cook and Moe Heideman. Friends may call at the Dods & McNair Funeral Home & Chapel, 21 First St., Orangeville on Monday from 2-4 and 7-9 p.m. Funeral Service will be held in the Dods & McNair Chapel on Tuesday, February 6, 2007 at 1:00 p.m. As expressions of sympathy donations to the Hockley Valley Bible Chapel would be appreciated. A tree will be planted in memory of Olive in the Dods & McNair Memorial Forest at the Island Lake Conservation Area, Orangeville. A dedication service will be held on Sunday, September 9th, 2007 at 2:30 p.m. (Condolences may be offered to the family at www.dodsandmcnair.com)

VERONIKA KINIO (NEE ZIERL)

Passed away peacefully, at Princess Margaret Hospital on Saturday, February 3, 2007, at the ...

LEE, Margery Dorothy — Star short-stop player of the Sunnyside Ladies Fastball League, who represented Canada at the Ladies World Fastball Championship in the 1950's. Passed away surrounded by her loving family after a brief illness on Friday, February 2, 2007, at the Trillium Health Centre, Mississauga. Margery, in her 80th year, beloved wife of Elmer. Loving mother of John and his wife Sharon, Heather, and Gordon and his wife Dianne. Dear grandmother of David, Jason, Andrew, Jennah, Robert, Patrick, Lora and Lisa, and great-grandmother of Johnathan, Katelin, and Alexandra, Carter, Cassidy, Emily and Kevin. Predeceased by her dear brothers Ronald and Wayne Robertson. Always remembered by many nieces and nephews. Friends may call at the Turner & Porter "Peel" Chapel, 2180 Hurontario St., Mississauga (Hwy. 10, N. of QEW) from 2-4 and 7-9 p.m. on Monday. Funeral Service will be held in the Chapel on Tuesday, February 6, 2007 at 11:00 a.m. Cremation. For those who wish, donations may be made to the charity of your choice.

Turner & Porter

LETIZIA, Giancarlo — Born September 3, 1937, Rome, Italy, passed away February 2, 2007, Toronto, Canada. Peacefully, in his home at the age of 69. Beloved son of Giovanni and Giulia Letizia. Forever remembered by his cousins Amedeo and Grazia Checcacci and their children Francesco and Chiara, cousins, Laura and Ferdinando Monteruschi and their children Paolo and Claudia. He will be sadly missed by his friends in Canada. Giancarlo came to Canada in 1969 and worked for Alitalia Airlines both in Montreal and Toronto for many years. Relatives and friends will be received at Bernardo Funeral Home, 2960 Dufferin St., (2 streets south of Lawrence Ave.), on Tuesday February 6 from 5-9 p.m. with a service in the funeral home at 8 p.m. Interment Rome, Italy.

LEUNG, Wei-Jin — Peacefully on Saturday, February 3, 2007 at Kennedy Lodge, Toronto, in her 100th year. Loving mother of Cowan Kue Hem and his wife Sheila. Cherished grandmother of Anna (Lester Chan), William (Carolyn) and Wilson. Dear sister of Jackson Wong and Silvana Li. Family wishes to express their heartfelt appreciation to the staff at Kennedy Lodge for their excellent care. Funeral service will be held Saturday, February 10, 2007 at PINE HILLS VISITATION, CHAPEL AND RECEPTION CENTRE, [...]

HAMM, Michael "Mike" — The family is saddened to announce the passing of Mike on Thursday, February 1, 2007 at the age of 55. Beloved husband of Gail (nee Irwin). Loving father of Christine and Shannon Hamm. Dear son of Peter and the late Peggy Hamm. Will be missed by his sister Susan Ritchie and her husband Joan Wrighton of London and his brother Jeff and his wife Lynne of Burlington. Nephew of Vera Hamm and Nick Hamm, both of Leamington. Loving uncle of Amy Jones and her husband Rob, Meagan Barlow-Hamm, Krystal Hamm and Korey Barlow-Hamm, Brother-in-law of Marilyn Westhoue and her husband Barry. Visitation will be held at SMITH'S FUNERAL HOME 1167 Guelph Line, (one stoplight north of QEW) BURLINGTON (905-632-3333) on Monday from 3-5 and 7-9 p.m. where a Funeral Service will take place on Tuesday, February 6, 2007 at 1 p.m. Cremation to take place. If desired, expressions of sympathy to the Alzheimer Foundation would be greatly appreciated by the family.
www.smithfh.com

HAMP, Robert F. — Peacefully on Saturday, February 3, 2007 at the Toronto General Hospital at the age of 89. Robert, beloved husband of the late Ethel. Dear father of Robert and his wife Bonnie. Loving grandfather of Christina. Robert will also be sadly missed by his other relatives and friends. Friends may call at the "EGLINTON CHAPEL" of the MCDOUGALL & BROWN FUNERAL HOMES 1812 Eglinton Ave. West (at Dufferin St.) 416-782-1197 on Monday from 7-9 p.m. Complete funeral service to be held in the chapel on Tuesday at 11 a.m. In lieu of flowers donations to the Heart and Stroke Foundation or the Kidney Foundation would be greatly appreciated.

HARDING, George Arthur — Passed away peacefully on Friday, February 2, 2007 with his beloved wife Marilyn by his side. Cherished father of Craig (Joyce), Cathy (Rod Pipher), Jennifer (Rob Fair), Lisa (Jerry Babin), Nicholas and Christopher. Proud grandfather of Stephen, Kelly, Joel, Dawn, Michael and Morgan. Loving brother to Dorothy, Joan, Diane and Linda. George will be missed by his brother in-law Craig Bull and sister-in-law Mary O'Regan, many nieces, nephews, cousins and friends. He will be greatly missed by the "fourth brother" Ken Lilley as George is re-united with his dear brothers Jack and Bob. Resting at Chapel Ridge Funeral Home, 8911Woodbine Ave., Markham (4 lights north of Hwy. 7) 905-305-8508. Visitation will be held on Monday, February 5th, from 2-4 and 6-8 p.m. Funeral Mass will be on Tuesday at 1:00 p.m. at St. Patrick's Church, 5633 Hwy.7 East. Cremation.

Chapel Ridge

HEMBREY, John "Jack" — Suddenly, at the Northumberland Hills Hospital in Cobourg, on Thursday, February 1, 2007. Jack Hembrey, at 85 years of age. Beloved husband of Joan Hembrey (nee Lynn). Dear father of John Hembrey (Gail), Julie Dodd, and Janet Stubbs (Chris). Cherished grandfather of Jessica, Jonathan, Sharj, Amy and Leila. Brother of Joan Stevens. Cremation with a memorial reception to be held at the Woodlawn Inn (420 Division St., in Cobourg) on Saturday, February 10th from 1 to 4 p.m. Those wishing may [...]

February 5, 2007 from 2-4 and 7-9 p.m. Funeral Service to be held on Tuesday, February 6, 2007 in the Chapel at 2 p.m. Cremation to follow services. In Michael's memory, memorial donations may be made to the Charles H. Best Diabetes Centre or to the charity of choice. Online condolences can be made at www.lowandlow.ca

DOS SANTOS, Manuel —
(April 13, 1912 - February 3, 2007)
Of Uxbridge Avenue. Mass 9 a.m. today at St. Mary of the Angels Church to Prospect Cemetery.

RYAN & ODETTE LTD.
FUNERALS FOR LESS™
416-532-5965

GEORGE JAMES DOVEY

Peacefully at West Park Long Term Care Centre, in his 85th year. Predeceased by his first wife Shirley, and his second wife Doris. Loving father of Marie Dickie and her husband Dave, and Donald and his partner Susan. Devoted grandfather to Erin, Andrew, Amy and Shane. George retired from LaForge Industries and during his long career he made many lasting friendships. He was highly respected in his business field. He enjoyed writing and his family is fortunate to have his written memoires, poetry and short stories. His wit and sense of humour will be missed by all those who knew him. Our heartfelt gratitude to the staff of West Park LTCC for their devoted care and to his daily companion and special caregiver Marcia. Friends may call at LYNETT FUNERAL HOME, 3299 Dundas St. W. (one block east of Runnymede Rd.), on Tuesday from 2-4 and 7-9 p.m. Funeral Service will be from the funeral home Chapel on Wednesday, February 7, 2007 at 10:00 a.m., followed by burial at Assumption Cemetery in Mississauga. If desired, donations may be made to the Heart and Stroke Foundation.

DRURY, Victor — Suddenly and peacefully at Rouge Valley (Centenary) Health Centre on Sunday, February 4, 2007 in his 80th year. Beloved husband of Ellen (Colton) and dear father of Craig Harvey (Paula). Brother of Anne Galea, Eva Thompson, Ronald and the late Clayton Drury. Also remembered by his nieces, nephews, relatives and friends. Friends will be received at DIXON-GARLAND FUNERAL HOME, 166 Main St. N. (Markham Rd.) Markham on Wednesday from 2-4 and 7-9 p.m. Funeral service in the chapel on Thursday at 11 a.m. Cremation. In lieu of flowers, donations to the Canadian Diabetes Association or the charity of your choice.

D'SOUZA, Innocent — Peacefully passed away with his family by his side on February 3, 2007 at Mount [...]

---

the Oakville Trafalgar Memorial Hospital, at the age of 86. Beloved wife of the late Louis Firkaly. Loving mother of Rosanne and her husband Ted Bateman. Sadly missed by her sisters: Helen Stratton, Marion Yuhasz, and her brothers: George Szucs, Andrew Szucs, Frank Szucs and Louis Szucs. Predeceased by her sister Kristine Meszaros. Rose was raised in Saskatchewan, moved to Montreal and in later years, she moved to the Okanagan Valley and subsequently to Oakville. The family wishes to extend a special thank you to the doctors and nurses of the Emergency Unit of O.T.M.H., and to E.M.S. Halton for their compassion and care. A Memorial Visitation will be held at the Ward Funeral Home, 109 Reynolds St., Oakville, 905-844-3221 on Wednesday from 2-4 and 7-9 p.m. A Memorial Service will be held in the Ward Chapel on Thursday, February 8, 2007 at 11 a.m. In lieu of flowers, donations may be made to Oakville Trafalgar Memorial Hospital or to Ian Anderson House.

FORAN, John "Jack" — (Veteran WW II)
Passed away peacefully on Saturday, February 3, 2007 at the age of 87. Beloved husband of Dorothy. Much loved father of Therese (Wendrick Yee), Cathy (Chris Fang), Patrick, and Maureen (Dan Van Damme). Loving grandfather of Cailyn, Noelle, Chanel, Emma, Aidan, Abby, Dylan and Julia. Dear brother of Valerie, Bryan, Elmer, John, and the late Patrick, Lamar, Joe and Thomas. Son of the late Peter and Ida Foran. Jack was a gentle man with a welcoming smile and a great sense of humour. Friends may call at the Turner & Porter Butler Chapel, 4933 Dundas St. W. (between Islington and Kipling Aves.) on Tuesday from 2-4 and 7-9 p.m. Funeral Mass to be held at St. Gregory's Roman Catholic Church, 122 Rathburn Rd. on Wednesday, February 7, 2007 at 10 a.m. For those who wish, memorial donations may be made to the Alzheimer Society or to the Heart and Stroke Foundation.

Turner & Porter

FREEMAN, Jean Evelyn — (Retired employee Greey Mixing Equipment). Peacefully at Simcoe Manor, Beeton, on Friday, February 2nd, 2007. Jean Freeman, in her 84th year, formerly of Caboto Terrace, Dufferin Street, Toronto. Loving mother of Gail and her husband Michael Ronan, of Tottenham, Nigel and the late Bert Freeman and Michael and Maxine Freeman, all of England. Loved by her 7 grandchildren, 4 great-grandchildren and predeceased by her granddaughter Kerry. Cremation has taken place. For visitation and memorial service details, please see www.rodabramsfuneralhome.com

GOODING, Harold (Ike) — Peacefully on February 2nd, 2007 at the Toronto East General Hospital. Harold, loving husband of Doreen; devoted father to Cheryl (Warren Tingle); proud grandfather to Colin (Colline) and Christopher Theodoru and Samantha Tingle. Harold was an employee of Christie's Bakery for 44 years. Family and friends will be received at PINE HILLS CEMETERY, VISITATION, CHAPEL AND RECEPTION CENTRE, 625 Birchmount Road (north of St. Clair Ave East). 416-261-8229, Saturday, February 17th [...]

Pilot of fabled Spitfire among first at D-Day

Toronto man flew 75 missions over enemy territory from 1940-44

MICHELE HENRY
STAFF REPORTER

The cockpit cover flew off. The wind lashed his exposed head and face. And Ian Keltie felt like he'd been "hit with a hammer."

Keltie, a pilot barely 22 years old and fighting for Canada in World War II, struggled to assess the damage to himself and his aircraft during that mission on Aug. 24, 1942.

He was escorting American B-17 bombers on a daylight raid of a target in France. He was under attack.

"I took violent evasive action and climbed hard and fast," Keltie wrote in *Spitfire II*, a book about Canadian fighter pilots published in 1999.

But as he mounted his defence and tried to retreat from the German enemy, he was careful not to turn his gaze too far to either side, into the wind.

"He didn't want to lose his sunglasses," Ross Keltie, Ian's son, said yesterday from his Toronto home.

"He had brand new sunglasses. They cost him two weeks' pay.

He was always like that."

Ian George Secord Keltie died in Toronto on Jan. 29. He was 86.

Known to his family as "Grampie," Keltie is believed to have been one of the few surviving Canadians to have flown a Spitfire. With a Rolls-Royce engine, he'd been "hit with a hammer."

Keltie, a pilot barely 22 years old and fighting for Canada in World War II, struggled to assess the damage to himself and his aircraft during that mission on Aug. 24, 1942.

He flew under Billy Bishop, who was Canada's highest-scoring fighter pilot in World War I. As a fighter pilot with the Royal

'I took violent evasive action and climbed hard and fast'

Ian Keltie, writing in Spitfire II, a 1999 book about fighter pilots

Canadian Air Force, 402 Winnipeg Squadron, Keltie flew 75 missions over enemy territory between 1940 and 1944.

He was the second pilot to land in Normandy on D-Day, Ross says, noting his dad told him the first plane plowed into a farmer. Keltie flew in support of the Dunkirk evacuations in 1940.

King George VI awarded him the Distinguished Flying Cross at Buckingham Palace.

Throughout his life, Keltie loved to travel and spend time with family.

A modest man, he rarely talked about his life during the war,

back to England," Ross Keltie, 53, said. "That was the safest thing to do."

"He kept heading in on him. Black smoke erupted into the air.

He opened fire on one of the two German Fw190 planes that he could see were closing

Keltie was halfway over the English Channel when his plane was hit. His leg was numb, he wrote in *Spitfire II*, so he wasn't in too much pain.

Keltie flew low over English land, praying enemy planes would retreat for fear of being hit by ground troops.

Within minutes he landed on the base. Shrapnel had hit him in the leg. His boot was full of blood.

After three weeks in the hospital, Ross Keltie said, his father was back in the cockpit of his Spitfire, which had the spunky cartoon sailor Popeye painted on its nose.

The eldest of five children, Ian day.

barely telling his children about his missions.

Ross Keltie knew little about how his father was wounded that "hot" day in 1942 on the flight back to Kenley air force base in southern England.

"He'd tell parts of the stories," Ross Keltie said. "We'd have to squeeze it out of him."

53, said. "That was the safest

Keltie was born May 26, 1920, in Millet, Alta. The son of a farmer who served in a Scottish cavalry regiment in World War I, Keltie joined the air force in 1939.

He was 19, fearless and raring to go.

"He always wanted to fly," Ross Keltie said.

Keltie grew up on a farm before moving to Edmonton to attend high school with his siblings. When he finished his studies the war broke out.

He returned to Edmonton shortly thereafter and married June Martin, who died 14 years ago at the age of 69.

For a while he worked as a bush pilot. After that he sold life insurance, then spent 25 years as a distributor of floor coverings. He flew a plane out of Toronto's Island airport until he was in his 50s.

Keltie was proud of his role in the air force. He let his children play dress-up with his uniforms, even if he wasn't able to talk about his experiences.

Ross Keltie had plans to ask his dad for more stories.

"You keep putting it off and then it's too late," he said.

Ian Keltie leaves his three children — Heather Sloan, Margot Dobson and Ross — seven grandchildren and a great-grandchild, who was born Friday.

A close-up of the nose of Ian Keltie's Spitfire IX, EN 398, showing "Popeye." The nose art was no longer on the aircraft when it was received by W/C J.E. "Johnnie" Johnson. — courtesy Steve Sauvé

was starting to turn to get on my back, so I thought it wisest to just keep going.

Meantime, I could hear my squadron mate Eric Bland saying on his radio that he was being shot at by FW 190s. He was right on the water near the English coast. But he evaded them, and we both landed at our base at Kenley at about the same time. He was badly hurt, and I felt for him. My flying boot was full of blood, so I was rather amazed that I was still able to stand. The 402 had an ambulance, one of three squadron vehicles supplied by the city of Winnipeg, which had adopted the squadron. The ambulance took us to the mess, and a little while later an RAF ambulance took us to an emergency hospital. It was in the wing of an insane asylum that was down the hill from Kenley airport, so we had to laugh about our new quarters. We were then transferred to the RAF Hospital at Cranwell, and I was back on operations a few weeks later.

That day I was flying a Spit IX, coded AE-B, but I also flew several other spitfires. In June 1942 my usual aircraft was a Mark V, BM 230, coded AE-T, and named *Gerfalcon II* with a full, not clipped wing, as some were later on. From February to March 1943 I had a Mark IX, coded AE-I in

February, and AE-B in March, which was serial EN 398. Someone in the ground crew, I believe, painted a large Popeye cartoon figure on the nose, so it was quite distinctive. Later on I discovered that it became even more famous as the mount of Johnnie Johnson, when he led the Kenley Wing just after that, with his initials on it JEJ. Several of our Spitfires carried Disney cartoon characters on the nose, quite large, such as the one of Goofy. I recall there were others, but whether they had any significance for the pilots or ground crew, other than just being for fun, I don't know.

On February 26, 1943, while on a fighter-bomber operation, I was flying EN 398, AE-I, when I damaged another FW 190 at 35,000 feet over Le Touquet, France. I was following Squadron Leader Bud Malloy. Climbing into the sun, we saw three FW 190s above, seemingly doing aerobatics. One did a roll off the top, coming down as if to attack me head on. I turned towards him, and climbed. I got a short burst into the 190, and he rolled over on his back, and went into a steep dive. After this I fogged over, and was unable to see much other than bluish-white smoke emitting from the Focke-Wulf as he went into a steep spin.

The next day, February 27, 1943, I was flying

the same aircraft again, when we ran into more FW 190s over Dunkirk. Lorne Cameron in his aircraft (BS 152, AE-W) shot down an FW 190, and two other fellows in our squadron also had scores (Gimbel and Ford).

On March 1, 1943, EN 398 was recoded AE-B for some reason. During that month we had several scrambles to chase incoming unidentified enemy aircraft, but we either found no one, or the enemy aircraft returned early. On March 7, I was on a rodeo to Berck-Oraulines, and then on the 8th, I was on a ramrod to St. Lo again in EN 398, AE-B, escorting sixty Flying Fortresses. I saw two FW 190s, but they were intercepted by 403 Squadron.

The activity was constant. The next day was a rodeo to Le Touquet, and again I saw an FW 190, but did not get close enough to engage. On March 13 I was on a circus to Amiens in EN 398 with seventy Fortresses.

Just over a year later, I was flying as OC of A Flight in 442 Squadron, under Dal Russel. I flew Y2-I for the most part, recorded as serial MK 729 in my logbook, including D-day, June 6, 1944, and I do remember the mass of ships. Just prior to D-day, my logbook records that we destroyed a giant Wurzburg radar installation in strafing attacks, and that we also dive-bombed V-1 sites. On June 10, 1944, I landed Y2-I for the first time in France, at B-3 airfield. On June 16, 1944, based at St. Croix sur Mer, I was bounced by an enemy fighter as I was taking off. I had a squirt, but did not detect any result.

After that, I wanted something different to do, and I ended up flying Liberator four-engine B 24 aircraft in 168 Squadron, at Rockcliffe, Ontario. I also flew Mitchells and C 47s, quite a bit of a change from single-engine Spits, and I don't think you see some of the aircraft I flew in too many logbooks of fighter pilots!

F/L E.A. Bland of Calgary in his Spitfire V, BM 509. — RCAF photo PL 10396

A lot of fine artwork showed up on 402 Squadron Spitfires. Here is "Goofy" on a Spitfire IX, AE-G, BS 353, flown by Norm Keene and others in 1943.

W/C J.E. "Johnnie" Johnson with his Spitfire IX, JE-J (Jr.), at Normandy. — courtesy Len Thorne

RAMROD 95

J. E. "Johnnie" Johnson

On June 15, 1943, I was leading the Kenley Wing (403 and 421 RCAF Squadrons) in my aircraft EN 398 (JEJ) on Ramrod 95. We were to escort Fortresses coming back from St. Bernay Aerodrome. We met other Spitfire wings off Fecamp at 27,000 feet, and almost immediately afterwards operations called up and said that the bombers were returning alright, so we could carry out a shallow penetration ourselves at my discretion.

There was a lot of high cumulous cloud, giving poor visibility, and as there was little in the Rouen area, I decided to fly in that direction. Operations then told me that bandits were climbing over Rouen, and flying west.

I set a course to intercept these bandits, and flew at 24,000 feet in order to avoid making contrails that would give us away. Shortly afterwards, we saw fifteen FW 190s flying towards the coast in line abreast.

I ordered 421 to remain top guard and led 403 to attack. I myself attacked the starboard 190 with cannon and machine gun, closing to 200 yards. I registered several strikes on this enemy aircraft, which pulled violently upwards almost into a stall. He jettisoned his hood, and I saw the pilot drop out, but I did not see his parachute open.

I then saw a further fifteen FW 190s on my port side, and they had gone into line astern — all turning to port very slowly, and covering about two miles. I closed in on the last enemy aircraft, and attacked him from port astern, closing to good range. I registered several cannon strikes, and pieces flew off the 190. As he went into a slow spin, his magazine in the starboard wing appeared to explode, and huge pieces of fuselage and wing were blown off. He was soon completely enveloped in black smoke.

In a few brief moments, I had destroyed two FW 190s. S/Lt. Hugh Godefroy (flying MA 467, KH-L) also shot one down, and F/Lt. H. D. MacDonald (flying BS 534, KH-M) got a damaged. The odds had been against us, but my Canadian squadrons had suffered no losses.

SEPTEMBER 19, 1943

Victor Haw, 411 Squadron

SUNDAY, SEPTEMBER 19, 1943, was a bright sunny day, as 411 Squadron taxied out for takeoff to escort American Marauders on a bombing mission. The target was the Lille marshalling yards in France. Our squadron, part of 126 Wing, was doing close escort to the bombers on that day, and I was flying number four in Blue Section in a Spit V B BL 422, as "tail-end Charlie." We flew east from our airfield, climbing to 12,000 feet, in order to rendezvous with the Americans over Ashford, Kent, in southeastern England. I was feeling quite well with the world, and apart from a certain tightness in the stomach that was always present on operations, there was no premonition of events to come.

We arrived over Ashford, but there were no Marauders, which left us with nothing to do but fly in circles until they arrived. Finally after circling for fifteen to twenty minutes and beginning to worry about fuel consumption, we joined up with the bombers and took our position on their flank and proceeded east across the Channel towards Lille. Shortly after crossing the French coast, one of the bombers developed engine trouble and had to turn back. Red Three and Four were ordered to return with the bomber, which left a large gap between Blue and Yellow Sections (squadrons flew in three sections of four aircraft each, in line astern — designated as blue, red and yellow, with red in the centre).

The wing carried on towards Lille, but by this time clouds had begun to form above us, which placed the bombers in a vulnerable position for attacks by German fighters. Because of this situation, the wing commander (Dal Russel) ordered the bombers to abort the mission and return to base. However, one of the bomber squadrons was determined to carry on, and our squadron had to accompany it. But the clouds became too low for a bombing run and so all bombers had to turn back along with the fighter escort. We had just turned toward the coast when four 190s were spotted,

climbing fast to our rear. In fact they were at five o'clock to my position as Blue Four, and had begun to open fire. I was feeling very uncomfortable when the squadron leader (Matheson) ordered a break, meaning all aircraft were to turn 180 degrees into the attacking enemy.

Since the break didn't indicate in which direction, I broke starboard into the 190s, which were still at five o'clock to me. All other 411 aircraft, as far as I could see, broke port, leaving me on my own. I found myself flying in a head-on attack with a 190. I recall vividly seeing the flame of his 20 mm cannon firing from the roots of his wing as we approached each other. I pressed the firing button of my guns (two 20 mm cannons and four 303 machine guns) as we attacked nose to nose at a combined speed of about 600 mph. He passed above me at very close range, and I pulled around with the hope of joining the rest of my section. I had just straightened out when I saw three aircraft that I assumed were my Blue Section, with 190s coming up fast to their rear. I opened fire on them without any visible effect, but at that moment I heard a very loud bang behind me, and on looking around saw that my radio equipment was a tangled mess, and that four 190s were on my tail.

I then broke into them, and we went around in circles for a few minutes, during which a large hole appeared in my wing close to the fuselage. Knowing there was no future in going around in ever-decreasing circles, I flipped my plane over in the opposite direction and headed for the ground.

I had hoped to get away at tree-top height, but found that when I reached ground level I had no idea in which direction I was flying, as there was no sun to guide me and all my instruments were awry because of the violent manoeuvres I had just gone through. I tried to orient my compass, but in order to do so I had to fly straight and level for a short period. This proved fatal, as I once again found myself the target of the four FW 190s.

Black smoke and flame began to flow from my exhaust, and the engine was coughing badly, indicating I wouldn't be airborne much longer. I pulled up sharply to gain height for a bail-out, and when I reached the point of stall I pulled the emergency release to jettison the hood. Nothing happened. It was with some feeling of resignation at that point that I realized that there was nothing else left that I could do. When the aircraft shuddered and began to fall away, the hood suddenly fell away, and I immediately dove over the side. There was a fleeting moment when I looked back and saw four FW 190s coming behind me, the leading one still firing.

As I went over the side, I pulled the ring of my parachute, and as it billowed out, I attempted to stop the back and forth swinging by pulling on the shrouds. But I hit the ground almost immediately.

As we had been briefed beforehand, I attempted to hide my chute by throwing leaves on it from the vegetation I had landed in (it was a turnip or sugar beet field). In the process of doing this I heard a noise behind me, and on turning saw a number of people watching me from over a fence. Since my efforts were obviously futile, I stood up to get away, but immediately fell and found I couldn't walk because of a badly sprained or broken ankle. Two people came across to help me, and we went into a nearby house. Shortly after, German soldiers arrived, and I was taken to a police cell in a local town. On the way we stopped where my burned-out plane had hit a barn, killing a cow. In general, I was well treated by the Germans. A doctor attended my ankle, and after several days with a few stops another POW and I ended up at the Frankfurt Interrogation Centre, where the treatment and conditions deteriorated.

An Un-Lucky Day Over Western France

Edward "Lucky" Likeness, 412 Squadron

"My ENGINE HAS BEEN HIT. It's packing up. I'm bailing out. Cheers chaps."

With these parting words over the radio transmitter my last operational flight over France came to an abrupt end on May 10, 1944.

Was it because I wasn't flying my personally assigned squadron Spitfire *Pistol Packin' Momma* (MJ 959, VZ-W)? It was grounded that day for scheduled maintenance, so I was flying MH 617, *Tiger Lady,* VZ-V — "Tex" Phillips's aircraft.

Our squadron was on a fighter sweep over western France in the Creil, Rheims and Laon area. We had been flying low, below 10,000 feet, for some time without encountering any German aircraft. Suddenly, our sister squadron (411) reported two FW 190s below, "on the deck," but soon lost sight of them. "Pappy" Crimmins, flying behind me, sighted them and dove in to attack. Then I saw them too, and dove some distance behind him. He got between the two planes, which were flying line astern, and immediately came under attack by the second one.

I closed in rapidly on the second one, and had just begun firing from about 150 yards when I was hit by cannon fire from a third 190 we hadn't seen up to that time.

The 190 I attacked exploded, and I flew through bits and pieces of it, at least one of which

Ed "Lucky" Likeness in his personal Spitfire IX, VZ-W, MJ 959, "Pistol Packin' Momma," in May 1944.

— courtesy Ed Likeness

hit the nose of my aircraft. My aircraft flipped onto its side, and I lost altitude sideways. My left wing had a large hole in it, and the aileron was mostly blown away. Pushing on as much right rudder and aileron as I could, I skidded upright and looked behind me for my attacker.

I saw him closing and crossing from above left, firing as he came. I pulled up hard into a half roll climb onto my back, and tried to pull down behind him. But the manoeuvre was sluggish; my engine had been damaged, and the power and control I needed wasn't there. I lost sight of him. I also lost sight of the rest of the squadron. There was not another aircraft visible in the sky.

Left to my own devices I gained what little altitude I could, and flew an emergency course for England. On checking the extent of the damage to my aircraft, I found a hole in the left wing completely obliterating the roundel. The two machine guns were bent up into the slipstream. The damage was caused by the cannon fire of the third 190 which attacked me. The pilot should get a cigar for that shot — it was literally a bull's-eye. Most of the left aileron was missing. The combination of these damages caused the aircraft to fly very heavy on the controls.

The constant speed unit in the propeller boss had been punctured, with a resultant uncontrollable pitch, and baptism of oil. The Pitot head was shot away, making my altimeter and airspeed indicator useless. The oil pressure had dropped to zero, and the temperature was above the danger mark. The glycol temperature was climbing noticeably. I turned off the oxygen as a precaution against cockpit fire should the engine explode, and glided down 1,000 feet to cool the oil and glycol.

I called the squadron commander, and as briefly as possible explained my plight. But he informed me not to expect any assistance until I reached the coast, as the squadron was split up, and coming out of France individually.

The prospect of flying alone over ninety miles of enemy territory to the coast, in a badly crippled aircraft, with a top speed of between 150 and 160 miles per hour, made me feel none too cheerful — and a bit lonely. The country was quite familiar to me, as many of my operations were over this particular part of France. I decided the tactic most likely to be successful was to keep my altitude and fly well around enemy aerodromes. On reaching the coastal flak belt, I would dive out when I saw where the guns were located. I could only hope for no more enemy fighter opposition.

It was one of those tranquil lullaby spring days — the kind when even the group captain will risk a few quick circuits around the aerodrome. The sun shone bright and warm in a cloudless sky; there was a slight haze over the Continent, but all the signs of winter had disappeared. Fields were green with growing crops, and the farmers were working the soil with that air of indifference so characteristic of them. Only the occasional farm wagon or bicycle put life on the roads that tacked to and fro across the country below.

During the next twenty minutes of flying — although at the time minutes seemed as long as hours — I was able to gain a little altitude. The highest I could get was 4,000 feet, but it meant sacrificing precious coolant temperature, which was above the recommended maximum now. I dared not attempt any further climbing. My arms were aching from holding the control column over, my right leg was stiff on the rudder bar, and my neck was raw and strained from looking for enemy fighters.

Like any other sinner who finds himself in an apparently hopeless position, I began to pray. I was already flying more on a prayer than a wing, and appreciated that nothing short of a miracle would see me safely through that flak belt.

If I could only reach England. If I could only reach the Channel. The thought of giving an air sea rescue squadron some business did not exactly appeal to me, but it was better than an "ending" in France.

Operations called and checked my position. I was only twenty-three miles from the French coast now. My spirits rose. I imagined myself Fortune's Favourite Child, everything was breaking right in the most astounding fashion. I flew on, expecting to welcome the sight of the coast at any moment.

I don't know if you have ever experienced that subconscious feeling which seems to shiper that you are going to catch hell. It came upon me all of a sudden — there was a tense stillness like the prelude to a severe electrical storm.

It broke with a deafening explosion. Dirty brown boiling puffs of smoke appeared. They were all around me.

That first salvo of flak is still vividly photographed with a good sound track in my memory. I dove in the direction of the coast, weaving violently and fighting to keep the aircraft under control. Salvo after salvo followed me with undeserved accuracy. The perspiration was swashing my forehead and saturating my clothes. I could not help admiring the accuracy of the gunners below — they followed me everywhere, getting closer with each burst. I could feel the shrapnel pounding my aircraft, and big jagged ulcer-like holes appeared in the wings. The metal was tear-

ing and being carried away in the slipstream. The controls became light, and responded sluggishly.

A flak burst right in front of me made the aircraft stagger and shudder. I *felt* that one. The engine stopped. Fire licked out of the exhaust. The controls refused to respond as I operated them in an attempt to remain airborne. As I spiralled earthward, I unfastened my harness and attempted to climb out, but centrifugal force created by the aircraft's tight turn threw me back into my seat.

As a last resort (I was below 1,000 feet), I trimmed the aircraft fully nose heavy, then jammed the control column forward. The laws of aerodynamics will prove that there should have been no reaction. But I got one. I was lifted out of

On November 12, 1943, P/O H.W. Bowker was flying his Spitfire V, VZ-X, BL 425, on a rhubarb with Ed Likeness in AR 275, when Bowker was injured by flak. They made it back to base, but it was their last flight in Mark Vs. The squadron soon after converted to Mark IXs. — courtesy J. Melson

the cockpit, bounced off the tailplane, and found myself floating in space.

There was no time to enjoy the pleasant feeling. I pulled the ripcord. The parachute opened immediately with a resultant jolt that affected every part of my anatomy. I drifted down into France, swinging slightly and heading for the only tree in the large field below me. With little effort, I slid to one side, but did not attempt to stop the swing so close to the ground. Looking around quickly for an avenue of escape, I noticed a car parked on the road below with a civilian gent waving to me. Would he help me? I made up my mind to run to his car immediately I touched down. *Touched* down — I came tumbling down to earth like the delivery of a load of bricks.

"I'VE HAD IT"

After somersaulting several times along the ground I ended up in a tangle of arms, legs and shroud lines, and expressive idiomatic English. A sharp tap on the quick release ring freed me of the parachute harness, and with two rips the Mae West was off. Springing to my feet, I started to run towards the Frenchman, who had remained by his car, swinging his arms like a windmill caught in a gale. It was then I realized my ankles were injured; nevertheless I hobbled painfully across the field.

Dame Fortune looked down on "her favourite child" and frowned. An open car full of German soldiers sped over the crest of the hill, trailing a cloud of dust behind them. The Frenchman could not help me with the soldiers at hand. I turned and headed for a clump of trees on the far side of the field. My ankles were cruelly painful, every step was torture. The soldiers welcomed me to their newly acquired Lebensraum with a six gun salute — loaded. The bullets whined past me making that zir-r-r-up noise that Zanuk portrays so well in his western thrillers.

The crux of the situation was at hand: to continue hobbling toward the trees giving the Germans some target practice, or to give it up as a bad job?

In exactly 3/265ths of a second, my mind was made up. I dove into the short stubble and awaited my captors, who were only a few yards behind me. I could hear the clack-clack of the rifle bolts as they prepared another volley. They gathered around me in a close jabbering circle, pointing their guns right between my g.d. eyes in a most menacing manner.

How I hoped I had a kind face — the kind they liked and did not feel like spoiling with nasty bullet holes. It seems I did. They motioned me to stand up with *hands hoch* (that's German for stick 'em up). A short little pin-head wearing the Eastern Campaign Ribbon (denoting the wearer was on the Russian Front when Joe's boys beat the hell out of them) searched me. It was just once-over-lightly this search; I had nothing that interested them. I wondered if this was the only search I would get, because I was carrying a few articles that would be very useful to me when an opportunity for escape presented itself. Before long I learned a few points on searches in general.

My first conversation with the Germans is one that must be recorded, I still enjoy the memory.

A pot-bellied soldier with one silver button on his epaulette seemed to be the senior in charge. He came forward brandishing a tommy gun in a manner that suggested he had been tortured by Dillinger, or someone who knew tommy guns equally well. In harsh German he growled, "Sprechen zie deutsch?"

I answered as calmly as I could with my teeth chattering nervously, at the same time shaking my head in the negative, "No deutsch, Dope."

He understood, but undaunted, tried again. "Parlez en francaise?"

His French was worse than mine, and mine would not even pass on St. Catherine Street, Montreal, where the language is international. I shook my head again, replying, "Ditto again, Dope."

He tried once more, proving the typical German thoroughness, but this time it was more a statement than a question. It was simply, "You speak English."

I confirmed his statement, adding, "With a slight Canadian accent, but you can hardly notice it if I speak slowly."

He understood my affirmative head nodding, but my conversation, I fear, was corny humour wasted on him — or else he secretly listened to

British Prime Minister Winston Churchill is greeted by G/C Bill MacBrien upon his visit to 127 (Canadian) Wing in France, on July 23, 1944. The aircraft that brought him was a captured Feisler Storch, valued even by the Allies for its short take-off and landing ability.

— courtesy Len Thorne

Bob Hope's radio program and was not impressed with my wit.

He pointed toward the road and said "marsh," so I "marshed."

A group of some fifteen or twenty French peasants had gathered along the road to see what was causing all the excitement, and to pick up some material for their long winter fire-side stories.

There was a waist-high wire fence between the field we were in and the road. Two of the soldiers climbed over, and I was motioned to follow. Evidently Potbelly had given up trying to talk to me. All his orders were given in sign language, punctuated by a threatening stance with the tommy gun. You would be amazed at how simple it is to pick up this language, every sentence is so clear.

I tried to climb the fence, but the wire was none too taut. As I stepped on it, it forced my ankle against the sprain, causing me more pain than I was willing to bear. As I stepped down again the Pin-head with the "Rusky Gong" muttered something in German, and pushed me, not hard, but it was still an unnecessary push. I turned on him, forgetting for the moment the tommy guns trained on me. Fortunately Potbelly had seen the push and was rolling into action — on *my* side.

He tore him an awful strip off him, saying something about me being a "British offizer" and "verbotten." Pin-head did not like this, and his hatred of me multiplied visibly. He glared, took a firmer grip on his tommy gun and — and that was all he did, thank God.

But I still had to get over the fence.

I don't know what prompted me to do it, whether I realized it would be a painful job no matter how I went about it and wanted to get it over with quickly, or it may have been ostentation on my part to supply another paragraph for the story (of which I was the hero) that would be the gossip in many French cottages for the next couple of rainy nights. I hurdled the fence with one leap. Now this is not my prescription for how to treat sprained ankles, but it did get admiring smiles of approval from the crowd, especially when the next person, Potbelly, tried it and got stuck on the top, almost hamstringing himself.

Now I got a good look at the gent who had been waving to me before the Germans appeared. He was a young man, well dressed and intelligent looking. He flashed me a quick smile and an even quicker V for victory (it was too rapid a movement to have any other meaning). Whether he would have assisted or arrested me had the Germans not arrived so quickly, I still can't confidently say. It is a known fact that a good percentage of Frenchmen were playing or attempting to play both patriot and collaborator, depending upon the risk involved.

Potbelly assisted me to the car, threw my parachute on the floor at my feet, placed guards with tommy guns on either side of me, and one in the front seat facing me. He himself stood on the running board, and we drove off. I must have been a dangerous-looking character, or else Potbelly believed his own propaganda about all pilots being desperate gangsters, because four tommy gun equipped guards are sufficient to deal with at least ten unarmed men. And as we drove along I also noticed two motorcycles, one leading and one trailing our car, each with a soldier in the side car equipped with a tommy gun. I felt as though I was carrying the payroll!

We drove only a short distance along a gravel road, through rather open country to a country home that was being used as a local headquarters. I was ordered out in the language I now understood so well — a wave of the tommy gun — and directed into the house.

It was a two-storey brick building, erected about the time Joan of Arc was a belle of the ball. The roof was in a bad state of disrepair and the windows had a thick frosting of dust. A long verandah on the front looked tired, and the crooked pillars supporting its roof seemed to be vying with the Tower of Pisa for top honours for angle of inclination. The lilac hedge that encircled the grounds had not been trimmed in years, and what were at one time beautiful flower beds were now pregnant with what promised to be a bumper crop of potatoes and cabbages. Two soldiers who could have told personal stories of the Franco-Prussian War of 1870 were cultivating these victory (?) gardens. Four other soldiers who were undergraduates of the Hitler Youth Class of '44 were patrolling the grounds. They reminded me of my own days playing cops and robbers — I was about fourteen then, too.

I noticed on entering the house that, except for a small sitting room office just to the right of the door, all the other rooms were filthy. I was ushered into the *salle-a-manger*, a high-ceilinged room with an old-fashioned chandelier suspended in the centre. The walls were barren, the paper covering cracked and hanging loose in several places. Light-shaded squares indicated that at one time it had been decorated with framed pictures, but these had been removed to swell Germany's cultural stores.

Two pudgy blubberous Luftwaffe privates whose superfluous rolls of paunch betrayed a lazy inactive life, greeted me with fishy handshakes that I accepted merely to keep peace on the premises. When I had settled myself as comfortably as possible on an old worn horsehair armchair, the two feminine members of the house entered and studied me with obvious curiosity, many snickered whispers and more than a few what were meant to be pleasant smiles. The latter was a wasted effort. Obviously they had to put up with the two pudgy types for 24 hours, seven days a week, so *any masculine* change of sight would undoubtedly in their opinion be for the better — even me, in spite of bleached hair and blood.

Finally one of the guards popped up with the old question. "Sprechen zie deutsch?"

I shook my head, "No deutsch, Bub."

Then the short skinny wench asked with hopeful enthusiasm, "Parlez vous en francaise?"

Of all the bicycles in the world I have been forced to endure these were the most dilapidated: of all the obnoxious women I have seen and refused polite conversation, these went to the foot of the class. I answered her with a negative shake of my head and a curt "NO" that had more finality than that of Dad's refusing me the loan of the family car.

She and her "colleague" remained on the opposite side of the room, snickering and whispering. I refuse to entertain the thought of what they might have been discussing; minds like theirs could only run on a single track and that track would be on the shady side of a narrow street.

Pudgy made several attempts to converse with me in a combination French, German, and elaborate sign-language. I tried to discourage it at first, by appearing not to understand but he was so persistently and stupidly harmless I finally gave in. For a while at least it kept me amused and helped pass the time. He flapped his arms bird-wing fashion and pointed questioningly at me. This I interpreted to mean "are you a flyer?" I nodded my head but could not help laughing at how silly he looked, standing there with his arms flailing the air.

I will not try to describe the sign-language for the latter part of the conversation, suffice to say his signals were clear and easily understood. He told me to choose either of the two women and sleep with her, the officer coming to fetch me would not arrive for sometime. This was kind of him, but as I had already described the women and my opinion of them, you can readily understand at least two of my reasons for refusing his offer. The tall stout woman inquired why not, was I married? I thought I would deal with this touchy subject more tactfully and speedily by lying that I was. Pudgy did not see why this should be a deterrent, he had *three* wives and still accepted all offers along the line. The skinny woman was now sitting on Pudgy's knee — I could not see his hands for petticoat and skirt — carried the argument further by adding that although she was unmarried she had a child of her own, she suspected several of many to be its father, but that was a minor concern. If there had been any doubt in my mind up to this time about the characters of these women, this last bit of conversation definitely removed it. I refused any further discussion by truthfully implying that it was against my principles. My discussion put them in quite a jovial frame of mind — Pudgy, especially, was feeling Merry.

As though to prove the skinny woman's brazen confession, a little girl about five years of age — the kind so common on Uncle Alfred programs, reciting or tap dancing to the strains of "Sidewalks of New York" — walked shyly into the room. She put a finger in her mouth and concentrated her coy attention on me. But Damn those bitchy females! — One of them dragged the child over to me and tried to force her to sit on my knee and expected the attention Pudgy was giving her?

The personal Spitfire IX of F/L Ketterson, coded VZ-K, MJ 306, 412 Squadron. Ketterson was lost in this aircraft on March 4, 1944, after an engine failure, possibly due to flak damage. — RCAF official photo PL 28277

Where was that officer who was coming to fetch me? I now looked forward to him as my rescuer from this den of vice and iniquity.

But here was the squirming squealing child, and I was supposed to cuddle her like a fond parent. If ever a man suffered; it was mental as well as physical torture now. Please don't misunderstand me, I don't want to imply that I dislike children. On the contrary, I love them and hope some day to have several (well, two anyway) of my own, but after studying this little bastard I would rather have been given a python to play with — at least a python could only bite and mortally wound me, death would be sudden. I refused to risk dying slowly of some infectious disease — then too, there was the possibility that the youngster was not housebroken. The child screamed louder, I begged them to cut it out; the woman eventually took her away. My sigh of relief must have been heard way out in Kapuskasing.

By this time my ankles had swollen considerably and the sharp jabbing pains made me wince. I removed my flying boots and massaged them for a little relief. The guard inquired if they were "kaput," a German word covering a list of adjectives ranging from broken to bombed flat. In answer I merely shook my head and left it at that.

Pudgy and the skinny wench disappeared though the doorway at the back. The stout woman went to the kitchen leaving me with one guard and the child who had found a new source for amusement in a scrawny grey cat that was fat but not from over-eating.

Presently the stout woman appeared, placed a bowl of soup on the table and motioned me to eat. I was not hungry, so I managed "Merci beaucoup" and indicated that I did not desire any food but would appreciate a glass of water. The latter statement had them puzzled for a moment, but after I went through the motion of drinking and mentioning "l'eau" several times, they caught on. The guard informed me sternly, "Wasser? Kein wasser. Bier! Good soldiers drink beer!"

So beer was brought in. It was French beer, and I lost no time introducing it to my stomach. It could hardly be called palatable, it tasted like ginger ale and sulphur-water, but under the circumstances I was grateful for two small bottles of it. I refused to drink any more. I've learned through bitter experience that potent drinks are deceiving, and can not always be detected by taste alone. I could not know what tests during the next hours and days were in store for me but I felt certain they could be best surmounted with sober facilities. I deemed it advisable to abstain early, if necessary for the duration.

Escape, though several opportunities arose, was out of the question now. I could hobble only a few slow steps then sit down and rest.

At last my savior arrived in an open staff car. I must admit that though my first impression — and last — of the German enlisted man was the very lowest, it was not so of this officer. He was an elderly weather-beaten gent with a good physique and a warm smile. He carried himself like a real soldier in a manner that commanded respect, and his dress was indicative of a man who was tidy and meticulous both on and off duty. He would have been a credit to the Palace Guard — or could this polished turn-out have been in my honour? (I can dream, can't I?) I was glad to see he was a member of the Luftwaffe, the German Army officers are reputed to be "Gestapo-like" in their dealings with Allied airmen.

He stepped briskly into the room and clicked his heels smartly in typical Prussian style. Before I could get to my feet and pay him the compliment of a salute, he saluted me; a real salute, not the pawing of the air and a "heil." I returned the salute and accepted his firm handshake.

Realizing I was injured, he begged me in quite good English, "Please sit down, I see you are wounded. I am sorry."

When I was seated he inquired of my guards if I had been given anything to eat. They told him food was offered but I refused it saying I was not hungry.

He drew up a chair, seated himself, and asked my name. I replied, "Likeness, Flight Lieutenant Likeness of the Royal Canadian Air Force."

He introduced himself. "I am Oberleutnant Weber, I am pleased to meet you though I would prefer it under pleasanter circumstances; however, as the French say, c'est la guerre!"

I thanked him for the compliment.

He was concerned about my injuries but I

assured him the cuts on my hands and face were not as serious as the abundance of coagulated blood indicated, that I felt certain my ankles were at the worst only badly sprained, but I would be grateful if he would have a doctor examine and bind them for me. He promised to attend to it that afternoon.

To use an R.A.F. term, he was "quite a decent bloke."

He rose and stated slowly as though choosing his words carefully, "You will come with me, please. Can you walk or shall I have my men carry you?"

I told him I could walk provided he did not mind if I went slowly and was not required to walk too far.

He agreed, adding, "Yes, of course, take your time. We will get into my car and drive to my headquarters to fill out the necessary papers."

Sitting in the backseat of the car between two guards — with tommy guns — we drove only a short distance to the ack ack battery Weber commanded. It was spread over an open field, the guns in deep pits with only their long black muzzles showing above the ground. The driver took us slowly along the perimeter of the site while a movie camera mounted on a truck filmed us. The gun crews were standing on the edge of their pits, the majority wearing either the Eastern Campaign Ribbon or the Afrika Corps wrist band. Weber informed me that it was this, his battery, that had shot me down. Of all the flak posts in France, I had to pick on this seasoned crew! I deserved to be shot down.

Drawing my attention to the camera, he added, "We have pictures of you from the time you appeared flying along until you disappeared behind those trees in your parachute. Your aeroplane — a Spitfire, was it? — broke up before it hit the ground." (Wow! I'm glad I did not try to crashland it.)

As we passed the camera I noticed Weber raise his head proudly and smile, giving the camera some good profile and full-on shots of his face. Egotist? Not in the full sense of the word. By this time he has probably sat in a theatre with his best girl friend, and together watched his picture in the news-reel as the commentator gave out with "the efficient work of our gallant men at the front,

destroying these gangsters who murder our women and children in cold blood . . ." It may have even have qualified him for an Iron Cross or something.

I could not help musing how Copper would have enjoyed being in my position. She often admitted how she delighted in having her picture taken. I'm glad she does, their frequent enclosures in her letters to me are a pleasant reminder of the loveliness I am going home to.

We drew up in front of a camouflaged dug-out and I was ushered down a zig-zag stairway cut out of the earth, into a low-ceilinged room about twelve feet underground. Two beds, a table, chair and several boxes were the furnishings; light was supplied by a hissing "tilly lamp."

I sat on the bed while the "papers" were filled out. There was very little to this inquiry, merely name, number and rank, no questions of a military nature. Weber was quite a time at writing out a full report of the circumstances during which I was shot down and captured — his eyewitness account on the former and Potbelly's on the latter.

This completed, he said apologetically, "Of course you know I must search you. I will try not to be unpleasant — but it must be done."

He accepted my offer to assist by emptying my pockets and placing everything on the table — well, almost everything. When I had turned my pockets inside out he felt my clothing for hidden articles and, satisfied that I was concealing nothing, turned to the pile on the table. Then he divided after examination into two piles: One he said was personal property I could keep, the other would be confiscated. I got back more than I expected — my lighter and my watch *could* have been "privately" confiscated. After studying the picture of Copper that I was carrying, he asked if she was my wife, and seemed disappointed when I told him, unfortunately for me, she wasn't. He paid her a compliment by saying, "A very beautiful lady, you are lucky to have her."

How often I have heard this; how irrefutable it is: how totally I believe it.

The necessary forms completed, Web led the way out of the dugout. The cameraman took close-up candid shots while gunners gathered around with private cameras snapping shots for their albums. I should get a lot of free publicity in Germany through these — but I know it won't be complimentary.

At length we drove off and about ten minutes later entered a small, rather plain village with little activity. Our car turned in through an arched gate and drove across a courtyard past a stable, and around to the front door of a large stone house. I followed Weber up a short flight of steps across a narrow terrace into the building. At the end of a long wide hall we entered a spacious room. It was the library-sitting room of the house, but since the occupation by the Germans it served as the Orderly Room of this Headquarters. Clerks, busy on typewriters and at filing cabinets stopped to stare stupidly at me with their mouths hanging open. I could feel their anticipation; it was centred around me, but I had not the slightest idea what they expected, so I returned their stare with all the contempt I could muster.

In a bay window on the far side of the room sat a pasty-faced middle-aged Luftwaffe officer, with a typical indolent adjutants hauty expression, glaring at me. Here was something irregular in his daily routine, and he was averse to dealing with it. Without asking his permission, I helped myself to a chair and sat down to relieve my ankles that were growing more painful as the day wore on.

Weber experienced some difficulty, having to explain everything three or four times before the Adjutant became cognizant. The latter insisted on searching me even though he was aware I had been searched before. He found nothing. Producing several sheets of printed forms he busied himself filling them in, Weber supplying the necessary information. Later he fired a question at me in German, but I pretended not to understand. Weber interpreted it for me. It was, "What is your Squadron number and the name of your base?"

I refused to supply this information. The adjutant persisted, fumed, then threatened; when he realized it had no effect, he resigned himself to my "irregular" disturbance of his daily routine.

On my request, a doctor was summoned. He arrived presently but what a disappointment he was. Before ascertaining the nature and extent of my injuries, he opened his bag and busied himself in it. A chance look at its contents shook me.

From the look of the equipment I was not sure whether he was a doctor or a handyman come to repair the office plumbing. He gave me some large white pills to help me get to sleep that night, then instructed his assistant to wash the blood off my face and hands. When he saw they were only minor cuts he directed the assistant to dab on some iodine paste. Preparations were made to bandage me. I could visualize myself wrapped like an Egyptian mummy after these two clowns finished with me, so I told them "not to bother wrapping it up; I'll take it as it is." They started to argue but my prognostication, "Save your paper bandages; you'll need them for yourselves before the war is over" quietened them. The doctor then concentrated his attention on my ankles, feeling them and twisting them every way possible — and previously not possible — making them pain even more. When his inefficient experiments reached the limit of my endurance I stopped him. He grinned and informed me in very bad English they were not "kaput," no broken bones; that they would heal in time. I dug a roll of gauze out of his bag, bandaged my feet as well as I could and put my boots on before he could get any more silly ideas, like practicing toe-holds on me. I often wonder what his profession was in civil life; certainly not a medical doctor. Not a clumsier archaic quack ever handed out a salicylate pill.

By this time a truck had arrived to transport me further. I thanked the doctor (for what?), shook hands and thanked Weber for his tact and decency and left with my new guards who were armed with — that's right.

My new mode of conveyance was not exactly a first class carriage. It was a truck deriving its fuel from a large tank in the chassis that converted coal into a combustible mixture. An officer, an old man of forty-seven, rather dissipated with an advanced case of DT's rode up front with the driver. I felt he needed the comfort of that seat more than I and climbed into the back of the truck assisted by my guards. The cannons, machine guns and a few rounds of ammunition had been salvaged from my aircraft — this to prevent the more patriotic Frenchmen from getting revolutionary ideas along the lines of "a dead German is one less to put up with." The two guards rode in the rear of the truck with me, as we set out along the highway in an North Easterly direction.

We stopped in front of a dingy clapboard house on the main street of the first village we came to. Three young women were standing around the doorway, their very appearance advertised their occupation, hobby, war work — or call it any other fancy name you prefer; they were figurations who could not demand more than a few francs for their efforts at satisfying the lusts of certain classes of men.

To my surprise the officer accompanying our party went into the house with one of the women; the driver and one guard took the remaining two "up them stairs." Here undoubtedly was the cause of the officer's dissipated look and DT's. I was left in the truck with the one remaining guard who sat restlessly awaiting the return of one of his bawdy "brothers in (harlotry) arms"; he was next.

The three reappeared — prematurely I thought — the officer more dissipated than ever but smiling like a Chessy cat that had taken a course on can-opening and passed with honours on a tin of sardines. He explained to my guard that as it was getting late we could tarry here no longer. When this ribald old wreck who had waited so passionately realized what this meant, he looked like a little boy who had just heard that Santa Claus had just retired from business; as we drive off he became a soldier again and muttered a long list of maledictory phraseology that would have been a manifestation to any grand-eloquent tar.

But what about me? Did that infirm pre-adamite in the front seat not intend to figure me in the fun? Or did he suspect that I had no lustful desire for the services of one of the "ladies of the parlour"? I would have loved the opportunity of refusing — it would have been something equivalent to a rough translation of what I told a French Canadian wench one evening on Montreal's busiest street, when I refused her "my business." Considering the situation from all angles, that German officer was not a gentleman.

It was evening when we entered the town of Bienville along an old cobblestone street, the houses were battle-scarred and the people walking about were pictures of a nation that was feeling the horrors and hardships of total war. Their clothes were old and shoddy, children were barefooted although the weather was quite cold. Women moved along slowly carrying their shopping bags, each with an unwrapped loaf of bread, while the dull cluck, cluck of their wooden shoes beat a tom-tom-like death dance on the worn sidewalks. The very air of the place felt like the interior of a tomb. A body of soldiers marched along toward the barracks at the foot of the hill, the rhythmic tramp of their hob-nailed shoes on the hard stones cutting the sourdine atmosphere like sabre slashes.

Our truck came to a violent stop in front of a grey stone mansion quite removed from the street. It would appear the Germans fancy this type of building for their nefarious purposes. A high stone fence topped with barbed wire surrounded the lot. A small gate to the right of the padlocked main entrance was opened from the inside by a sentry. I dismounted from the truck and stopped into what must have been at one time, a beautiful terraced garden, but now through the lack of proper spade husbandry was an unsightly tangle of underbrush and weeds. The scarlet and white flag with the black double cross in the centre was flying from a pole on the roof.

The sentry directed me to the gatehouse just inside the wall. I limped along the path, up four steps, through a narrow doorway, and into my first German "jug."

RECOLLECTIONS

F/O (later S/Lt.) R. D. Forbes-Roberts, 416 Squadron

WHEN STEN LUNDBERG WAS HIT BY FLAK on May 21, 1944, I was preoccupied with a second attack on a train (flying Spitfire IX, MJ 953). Hearing Sten was hit, I radioed to him to fly south — mainly to get as far away as he could from the area, as there appeared to be a number of enemy troops below. I proceeded to finish my attack on the train. After the attack I hoped to contact Sten again, and at least escort him down or report what happened to him. Unfortunately, I and the others on the flight could not locate, see, or find any trace of Sten, other than to hear on the radio transmitter that he was going to bail out.

His fate was on my conscience for many years, as it was not until after the war that I found out that he survived. It may have appeared to Sten that we had abandoned him, as I was so intent on destroying the train, but we had hoped to rejoin him immediately afterwards. If I had known he was in serious trouble I would have broken off my attack on that old train. I am glad things turned out OK for Sten, in the end, and that he was able to endure his stay as a POW. The only notes in my logbook were that Sten had had an unlucky hit by flak, and that on this rhubarb we had "lots of fun train-busting."

The next day was a very exciting one, when a ranger I was leading (flying MK 207) shot up five trains, and then, when very low on fuel and ammo, we ran into six enemy aircraft near Etrepagne. During the melee we really lost all track of where we actually were. At any rate we did rather well, destroying five of the enemy, which were Me 109s, and not FW 190s as recorded in the book *Fifth Year*, an RCAF history. The other pilots were G. R. "Pat" Patterson (flying MJ 770), W. A. Palmer (flying MJ 575), Sandy Borland (MJ 874), and W. F. "Bill" Mason (MJ 347). Although I had

A Spitfire V from 416 Squardon, 1942. — photo by Phil Gofton

flown some 140 operational hours by then, it was the first time I had actually seen enemy aircraft close enough that the black crosses were very distinguishable.

Fortunately, with the help of the ground controllers back home, we all landed safely, very short of petrol, at Friston. One of the pilots had a piece of debris, plexiglass I believe, possibly from the hood of an Me 109, stuck in his radiator. When he landed it fell out, and his glycol coolant for the Merlin engine all ran out. While flying, the pressure from the air had held it in, otherwise he would have met the same fate as Sten the previous day.

Other than shooting up some enemy transport, and many hours of patrol of the beachheads, I had little activity until another engagement with the enemy on July 14, 1944. I was leading four of the pilots (flying MJ 838), when over our own airfield, B-2, we encountered more than fifty enemy Me 109s and FW 190s. I had a bit of a struggle keeping enemy aircraft off of Bill Mason's tail (flying MK 835), as well as my own. His aircraft was hit when the fifty-plus aircraft fired at us head-on, but he managed to carry out a wheels-up landing below on the strip. In climbing back up, I sighted one lone enemy aircraft, and wondered where all the others had gone. Anyhow, I was successful, and shot him down. I then pursued what may have been another, but I could not catch up.

When I returned I could not understand why our ground crew was so excited. They picked me up and carried me over to where there was a crowd standing around. It turned out that in the middle of the crowd was the German pilot of the FW 190 I had shot down. So I was able to meet him, but it was a brief encounter, since I was scrambled shortly after that on another mission. When I got back I was accused of grand-standing, with a few other barbs, all in good fun!

A brief footnote to this story would be the fact that the pilots on the wing made the captured pilot a very nice gesture. They passed around the Mae West life vest he wore, much like our own, so that he received virtually every pilot's autograph from the three squadrons that composed 127 Wing at that time. It came into my possession later on, and I have since sent it to the war museum in Ottawa.

I flew another thirty or forty hours on ops, until August 4, 1944. I had little more excitement to that time, when I was regretfully taken off operations, having completed over 200 hours. I ended up instructing at a Spitfire OTU for seven months. After a month's leave in Canada, I was on my way back. But the war was about to end, and just as I was boarding a ship to Halifax I received a cable advising me that my services were no longer required.

"The Good Shepherd"

On 29 November 1943, 401 and 412 Squadrons of the RCAF flying out of Biggin Hill escorted 72 B-26 Martin Marauders of the USAAF on "Ramrod 339," to bomb an enemy airfield at Chievres, France. Reaction from defending FW 190s of the German Luftwaffe was intense, and nearly all of the Canadians were involved in air combats.

On the way back, 401 Squadron Spitfire IX pilots F/L W.R. (Bill) McRae in YO-L, MJ 199, flying alongside F/L J. (Jack) Sheppard, DFC in YO-A, found one of the B-26 Marauders limping along and escorted the American bomber safely back to base.

The mission was a memorable one for Bill McRae, and the dramatic painting by Ron Lowry certainly shows a moment in time that was typical of the flying done by the Canadians flying Spitfires in World War II.

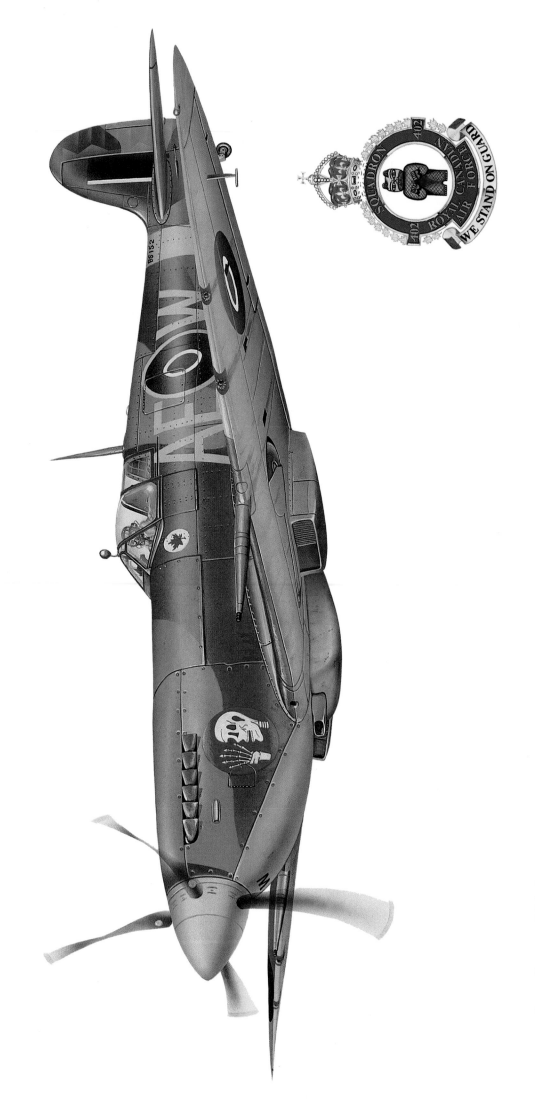

Lorne Cameron, DFC, from Roland, Manitoba flew this Spitfire IX, serial BS 152, in 402 Squadron, RCAF, early in 1943. The groundcrew have painted a variation of a skull and crossbones on the nose, possibly to denote the deadly prowess of the pilot, one of Canada's aces with six victories and two damaged to his credit.

One of the rather unsung heroes of the epic "Battle of Britain" in 1940 was ace pilot William Henry Nelson, DFC, from Montreal, Quebec. He actually won his DFC as a bomber pilot in the RAF, but switched to fighters and flew with 74 Squadron during the "Battle." He was killed in action on November 1, 1940.

Ian Keltie flew this Spitfire IX, EN 398, "Popeye," AE-B as his personal aircraft in 402 Squadron, February to March of 1943. The aircraft would soon become famous as the personal mount of British ace J. E. "Johnnie" Johnson, coded JE-J, when he led the Canadian Wing of Spitfires from Kenley.

Wing Commander Lloyd Vernon Chadburn was awarded the DSO and Bar, DFC, Croix de Guerre and the Chevalier of the Legion of Honour. He grew up in Aurora, Ontario, where he is remembered with a small museum. The painting depicts the personal aircraft of Canada's most popular Wing Commander, a Spitfire V, with his initials "LVC", serial EP 548, which he flew in 1943.

Spitfire XI, PM 133 on the metal-planked runway at B-90 Petit Brogel in Belgium, in April 1945. The spinner on this 400 Squadron aircraft was later painted a bright yellow. — RCAF via Steve Fochuk

Spitfire XI, again from 400 Squadron, at B-154, Luneburg, in May 1945. The high-altitude camouflage carried by these aircraft earned the squadron the nickname "The Bluebirds." Unlike 414 and 430 Squadrons, also part of 39 Recce Wing, 400 carried no guns, only cameras.

Opposite: P/O J. E. McRea is seated at the organ on a stack of jerry cans, and Padre S/L Crawford Scott conducts a Sunday service in July 1944. With a Spitfire IX, DN-Z, in the background, the congregation includes P/O W. H. Palmer, F/O M. R. Sharun, F/L D.W. Hayworth and F/O A. R. McFadden, all in 416 Squadron, RCAF.

— Photos RCAF via Steve Fochuk

Rod Smith, DFC and Bar, provided the details for this painting of his Spitfire V, which he flew at Malta in 126 Squadron, serial BR 471. Still in its tropical camouflage, widely used in the Middle East and North Africa, many of the Malta Spitfires were also repainted hastily in shades of blue for the combats they faced over the blue waters of the Mediterranean.

Guy Mott, DFC, an ace pilot in 441 Squadron, RCAF, went missing August 6, 1944, but evaded capture and returned to fly again. Joining the RAF postwar, he was armaments officer of the Kai-Tak Wing at Hong Kong, where he often flew this Spitfire 24, W2-L, in 80 Squadron. The black-and-white stripes were added when the Korean War broke out.

Richard (Dick) Audet, DFC and Bar, from Lethbridge, Alberta, Canada's "ace in one day," flew DB-G, MK 950, as his personal aircraft in 411 Squadron, RCAF. He had a total of 11½ victories in the air when he was shot down by flak on March 3, 1945.

Edward "Lucky" Likeness of 412 Squadron, RCAF, flew this Spitfire IX, VZ-W, MJ 959, in 1944. It was named "Pistol Packin' Momma," after a popular song of the day.

Wings awarded to Flt/Lt. Gilbert "Gib" R. Haldane, following air test on N/A Harvard 2B-2390 #2 S.F.T.S. Uplands. Most Spitfire pilots spent a lot of time flying Harvards in training. Often, after operational time in Spitfires, they returned to Harvards to train others. Haldane wanted very much to be a Spitfire pilot, but ended up in Lancasters instead. He once flew his "four-engine Spitfire," ground strafing like it was a fighter! This painting is included to show the aircraft in which so many spent so much of their time back in Canada.

Ace pilot Hugh C. Trainor, DS, DFC, with 8½ victories, was C. O. of 401 Squadron, when he was shot down on September 19, 1944. As an instructor in Canada, he also made waves flying an unauthorized souped-up Harvard trainer, with double the usual horsepower. It helped get his wish — to fly in an operation squadron overseas!

Previous Page: Famed artist Bob Hyndman in 411 Squadron, with Robert "Buck" McNair, another famous personality in the RCAF. McNair, DFC and two Bars, is credited with 16 victories and ended the war as a Wing Commander.

— Photos RCAF via Steve Fochuk

Spitfire XI, PM 151, flew with 400 Squadron, RCAF, from February to June 1945. It is shown at airfield B-90, Petit Brogel, in Belgium in April 1945. — RCAF official via Steve Fochuk

The gas tank of 414 Squadron RCAF Spitfire XIV FR, NH 757, is topped up prior to a sortie at Wunsdorf, Germany, in April 1945. Individual letter code for this aircraft was "D", and it was flown by several pilots, including by Dave McBride to photograph sites in Germany, during which combats ensued with the last remnants of the Luftwaffe.

— RCAF officail via Steve Fochuk

Ace Don C. "Chunky" Gordon shown sometime in March 1944. He scored 14½ victories with 442 Squadron, RCAF, in his Spitfire IX, PV 148, coded Y2-K. As a "Y2-K" project, in 1999, a Spitfire is being restored in British Columbia, Canada, in his honour. Born in Edmonton, Gordon grew up in Vancouver, B.C.

— RCAF official via Steve Fochuk

SALERNO — FRIENDLY FIRE

Bill Hockey

I JOINED 93 RAF SQUADRON in December 1942, about a month after the invasion of North Africa by the British and Americans. We were assigned the task of close support cover to the army, so as they pushed the enemy back, we moved ahead with them, provided we could establish a new landing strip. We moved our base camp once a month on average and operated from twenty-five different sites in Algeria, Tunisia, Malta, Sicily and Italy during the twelve months that I was with the squadron.

We arrived at our new base, a landing strip on the north coast of Sicily, on September 6, 1943. It was a really nice set-up, being about one hundred yards from a sandy beach where we could go swimming every day. The water was still warm, so we could swim any time we weren't flying.

Why we were here at Falcone we had no idea, except that we always followed the army, and since they had already started moving up the toe of the boot in Italy, we assumed we were moving along with them. Boy were we wrong, as the next morn-

ing two large lorries arrived and unloaded a whole bunch of ninety gallon belly tanks. Our ground crews immediately went to work fitting them to our Spits, but we still had no idea why and what for.

September 9. This morning at 6:30 A.M. we took off on the greatest task assigned to Spitfire squadrons. With ninety gallon tanks slung under our bellies we were to cover the Allied landings at Salerno, 170 miles over water from our base in Sicily. We did two patrols the first day but did not run into any enemy air activity. We did lose two kites due to prangs at our own landing strip.

We did only one patrol the next day — also uneventful — but were treated to an unrehearsed show by ten Spits from one of the carriers, who were told to land and refuel at our base. Having heard a lot about these carrier pilots, we sat ourselves down beside the landing strip and waited, though not for long. The first two came in quite fast, evidently expecting to hook on to the arresting cable (which we didn't have), and ended up

Bill Hockey sitting on the cockpit sill of his 93 Squadron Spitfire V, "Freckles."

in the olive orchard, not in the best of shape. The next six managed to get down safely, but the last two put on the best show. Number nine landed OK, but before he could get off the strip number ten came too fast and ran into him. The pilots got out all right but the planes burned up in the middle of our landing area.

By the third day the beachhead was well established, and we were preparing for takeoff with Squadron Leader MacDonald leading a flight of six. I was leading top cover with wingmen Sgt. Andrews and Sgt. Barker (his first flight with us). We only had the nine serviceable air craft and had no premonition of what was to befall us on this patrol.

About two hours after we were on patrol our base called to inform us that the squadron to take over from us did not have enough serviceable air craft to make the trip, and that we were to land at a strip the Americans had just made and they would refuel us. There were already a bunch of P 38s beside the landing area so we figured, great, we can have a chat with some of the pilots while we are being refueled.

After being on patrol for three hours, which was probably the longest time any of us had been in the cockpit for one trip, the CO announced we were going in to land. Unfortunately, our allies had other ideas, as the United States Navy opened up with all they could muster. Ray Baster was the first one hit, in the engine, and belly-landed beside an American field hospital. Next was Squadron Leader MacDonald. With wheels and flaps already down, they blew off his tail, and he crashed in flames.

When I witnessed that I took my two wingmen over the mountains, where the Germans were. They were either laughing too hard at our predicament or took pity on us, as they never bothered to fire at all. By this time, the other four had landed all right, but not without incident, as Richardson got a few machine gun rounds through his wings and Shanks got a fifty calibre through his ninety gallon tank.

It was a well-known practice to eject your belly tank if you got involved with enemy air craft or heavy flak, for better manoeuvrability, but mine wouldn't release. This was lucky for me, as I will elaborate. Andrews went over to land, and I wanted to check to see how Ray had made out so I dove down to 200 feet and waved to him as he stood beside his Spit, with about twenty American soldiers training their guns on him. "Pretty scary," he related the next day, when he got back to our base. As I pulled up from checking on Ray, I got hit in the fuselage with four, fifty calibre machine gun rounds, one of which ruptured the hydraulic line to my brakes, as I discovered on landing. Another exploded in my ninety gallon tank (which I quickly released) and spattered the backs of my legs with whatever was in the bottom of the cockpit. I was flying in short pants, for the first and only time, and the calves of my legs looked like I had the measles, with drops of blood sprouting out all over them. By the way, Sgt. Barker stuck with me the whole time and never got a scratch.

Due to my obvious lack of brakes F/Lt. Richardson suggested that I stay the night, but I said no way am I going to stay here with so many trigger-happy allies around. Anyway, after getting refueled and starting to taxi out for takeoff, I got a couple of American pilots to grab my wing tips and get me lined up straight. I got airborne all right and landed back at Falcone without incident, ground looping near the end of the strip. Andrews couldn't get his air craft started, so only six of us got back to Sicily.

When the boys saw the blood on the backs of my legs, they suggested I check in with our doctor, which I did. Luckily, after having me on a table for about half an hour, washing off the blood and picking out numerous particles of sand, he reported all clear — no shrapnel.

We kept patrolling the beachhead area for the next eight to ten days, then moved to a base in the area. One month later we were stationed in Naples, where I finished my tour of operations.

Spitfire V, EP 767, 411 Squadron, Digby, England. — courtesy Clerihew

Spitfire VZ-K, BL 259, in December 1941, in A-Flight of 412 Squadron. — Phot Credit D-Hist, via Steve Fochuk

DESERT WAR

E. A. "Bud" Ker, DFC

WHEN WORLD WAR II STARTED, I made a short trip from Fonthill, Ontario, to the recruiting centre in Niagara Falls. It would be an eventful few years for me.

On my first tour, I flew in 145 Squadron, in the RAF. As I recall, when I joined the squadron there were four Australians, two New Zealanders, three South Africans, and four Canadians, as well as the British. Our squadron leader was the remarkable American, Lance Wade, from Texas. Together, we were part of the Desert Air Force, chasing the enemy across, and finally out of Africa.

We were equipped with the Spitfire V B for most of my time with the squadron. I considered it very much the equal of the enemy aircraft we encountered. My usual aircraft was ZX-H. Later on we received the Mark IX, which was faster.

I recall one mission up around Cape Bond. There were six of us on the sweep. We sighted some Luftwaffe 190s, and two of us peeled off to see what was going on. They were down sun from us, so we didn't have to do much manoeuvering. We had a go at a couple of stragglers. The belly tank of the one I attacked blew up, and that was the end of him. My number two got a probable. We didn't stick around, as it didn't take long to use up our ammo.

The Italians also had their Macchi 202 fighters, which were very streamlined. I shot down one of these sleek aircraft on March 29, 1943. Early on the Italians seemed aggressive, but later on they did not seem very determined to oppose us.

By August 1943 I had shot down two Macchi 202s, destroyed one Me 109, and had six others listed as probables, or damaged. While we had cine-gun film in use during our air combats, it was not always possible to see what had happened, and we were often escorting other attacking aircraft, such as Kittyhawks, which it was our duty to protect. We also carried out a lot of bombing in our Spitfires.

Anyway, I was awarded the DFC, and sent back for a rest as an instructor in Canada at No. 1 OTU in Bagotville, Quebec. After that I started my second tour flying the magnificent Spitfire XIV in Europe. A promotion brought me to 401 Squadron, and I had some more air battles late in the war, when my usual aircraft was a Spit IX, MJ 340, YO-R. We did not see a lot of the Luftwaffe, and when we did we were often outnumbered. But we waded into them anyway. On one occasion several of the fellows got scores, but I used up all of my ammunition, and did not get a claim.

Most of our missions then were ground attack, against railways and motor transport. I often led the squadron at that stage of the war, and in fact, ended up as squadron leader just as the war ended. We continued on for a while on occupation duties into June and July 1945.

Opposite: Sgt. Pilot E.A. "Bud" Ker with his tropical Spitfire Vc, ZX-H, AB 277, at LG 154, Egypt, 145 Squadron, RAF, in July 1942.

GROUND CREW

Bill Roberts, 412 Squadron

I HAD BEEN IN THE ARMY, and when I received my discharge papers, I took them with me to the aircraft recruiter. The air force took them as proof of age, and I was overseas before my father went. I was seventeen going on eighteen years old.

I went to an RAF school for mechanics, and in 1941 I was in Cosford, going through an air mechanics update. I then started with 412 Squadron when they were formed in Yorkshire. They were at Merston, near Tangmere, when I joined them in 1942. I was wearing an RAF uniform, and had fairly easily acquired an English accent by that time, since my father had been English. I actually had trouble convincing people that I was Canadian!

The 412 Squadron was originally part of 11 Group, but when we became part of Second Tactical Air Force it put us in a different area. After that we were always in southern England, until the Invasion and D-day. I always looked after the CO's aircraft, so I looked after Keefer's aircraft, VZ-A. Keefer came to us at Perrenporth, in South Wales. At that time we were building up to D-day, with a practice called Operation Spartan. Keefer was well liked by the squadron, starting as a flight commander of A Flight, and becoming CO after we lost our squadron leader. He later returned to us after his tour, coming back as a wing commander.

I also looked after Johnnie Johnson's aircraft, JEJ, at Beny sur Mer. I can recall that Johnson was very fussy about who looked after his aircraft. He had to know you first. Johnson was not with us

Armourers at work on Spitfire YO-M of 401 Squadron. — courtesy Cecil Mann

Groundcrew gassing up 401 Squadron Spitfire IX, YO-S, MJ 565. — courtesy Cecil Mann

long, however, as he was in charge of other squadrons too.

Beurling was also on 412 Squadron for a while. But he was not a team player, as he seemed to be looking after himself, not thinking of the other pilots. He flew VZ-B, and his cousin, a fellow by the name of Gibson, was the only fellow he let near his aircraft.

Beurling was leading B Flight when he gave the order to switch from the slipper tanks to the other internal tanks, at under 500 feet. Because of condensation, it was not always a smooth transition, and this time it ended in disaster when one of them failed, and we lost a pilot. Since Beurling had given the order, and was flight leader, he got the blame. It gave him some difficulty with the squadron, so he was gone soon after that.

I left the squadron in Holland, actually near Vogel, and the squadron went into Germany after that. I went back to England at that time, as my tour was up. I had learned to fly the squadron's Gypsy Moth, and since I was keen to fly, Buck McNair suggested I should try out for pilot training. I showed some promise on the tests, but when it came time for the optical tests it was discovered

that I was short-sighted. This surprised me, since I didn't wear glasses, and didn't seem to need them, but that was the end of my flying career.

I worked on quite a few different versions of the Spitfire in my time. I can recall the difference it made when the Mark V A became the Mark V B, with the addition of the Stromberg-Carlston supercharger from the United States. The British were skeptical at first, as they are not noted for liking change. But what a difference it made. With the direct fuel injection of the new supercharger, the pilots could outfly the FW 190, or face it on more even terms. They made the change at maintenance units, before we got the aircraft, so you could not tell which aircraft had the new units until you got the cowl off. It made a big difference to the pilot who was going to fly the aircraft.

Later on, we received my favourite, the Mark IX Spitfire. It had more power, and it had even better superchargers.

As we were in the TAF, we were expected to be able to repair any kind of aircraft that might land on our bases, so we were given some training on other types of planes. One funny incident happened when I was running up a Typhoon airplane at full power. I remember how poorly I felt, owing to a cold. I was running a fever, passed out in the cockpit, and don't know how long the plane was running before somebody came and got me. It turned out to be another fellow with my name — Bill Roberts. He was called senior, and I was junior, since I was quite young then. Well, the Typhoon was huge compared to the Spitfire. He had to climb a ladder, get on the wing, and try to get the cockpit canopy open to get me out. At the time, my hand was on the throttle, and the plane could have taken off by itself! They managed to pull me out, and I spent some time in the hospital with a bad fever.

As a mechanic, it was a lot of work keeping the aircraft going. I've got the smashed fingers to prove it, but that's life. The Spitfire in particular was not designed from a maintenance point of view, but I understood that you have to have a certain aerodynamic shape. You haven't got room to swing a wrench — they were just straight spanners. We didn't have the kind of tools they have today, with all the swings, tilts, and adjustments, which would have helped enormously.

However, as far as I was concerned, the Spitfire was a beauty. Its appearance gave our pilots a lot of confidence, and we did our best to keep the aircraft in top shape.

George F. Beurling's 403 Squadron Spitfire IX. — courtesy Len Thorne

D-DAY "PEP TALK"

Cec Brown, 403 Squadron

IN JUNE 1944 I RECEIVED A NEW SPITFIRE IX, coded KH-N, serial NH 196. It was a good one, and I spent some time with my ground crew Mel and Johnnie, getting it fine-tuned. We soon had it flying beautifully, almost hands-off. In the first few days of June, I had only one operational flight, and it was uneventful. Tension was building up, however, as everyone realized that the Invasion was not far off. Our tents were near the main east-west highway and every night there was a steady procession of vehicles going towards South-hampton, an obvious embarkation point.

On the morning of June 4, we had begun painting broad white and black stripes on both wings at the wing root of our Spitfires. These were perhaps ten inches wide. About four or five similar stripes were painted around the fuselage, just forward of the tail assembly. It had been decided that all Allied aircraft would wear these stripes as identification. There were not enough ground crew to do all the aircraft, so we worked along with them to get the job done. To keep the stripes secret from the enemy, no operational flying was to be done after they were put on, until the Invasion.

On the evening of June 4, all pilots were called together to be told that D-day was to be June 5. The meeting was attended by 127, 126 and 144 Canadian Wings, all flying Spitfires. Johnnie Johnson, the British ace, had recently taken over the new 144 Wing. Up to then, I had never seen Johnnie, although his reputation was well-known to everyone.

The sector commander for 83 Group, Second TAF, was Air Marshal Harry Broadhurst. He was terribly jealous of Johnson's record and reputation, and while he outranked Johnnie, it was generally felt that Johnnie had more clout at Air Ministry than Broadhurst did.

On this occasion Broadhurst was giving the pep talk to all the pilots and made the mistake of saying, "I want you to give the supreme effort to your assignments for D-day. It is vitally important that every assignment be carried out to the fullest extent. If you should be called upon to carry out attacks on ground targets, I am willing to sacrifice a Spitfire and pilot for every ground target you can destroy."

Of course, Johnnie Johnson wasn't about to let him get away with it. He broke in with, "Sir, perhaps some of the pilots have difficulty in understanding just what you mean. Would you like to lead the first attacks and show the pilots, by example, just what you really mean?"

Broadhurst was furious, but Johnnie had put it so well that he could think of no reply.

Shortly after that, word came through that D-day had been postponed because of bad weather. That meant that we could not do any ops the next day. For reasons I cannot remember, I see from my logbook that on June 5 I took the group captain's old Mark V Spit, coded WR-M, up for a cannon test.

The tension became almost unbearable in the few days before D-day. The build-up of troops continued nightly, and everyone knew we would not have long to wait. We pilots were not overly concerned, since we were quite used to flying over enemy territory firing our guns, dive-bombing, and getting shot at. To us D-day would be just another operation, but on a scale much larger than we were used to, and involving hundreds of thousands of people, and thousands of vessels and equipment. None of us anticipated the immensity of what came to pass.

The delay on June 5 did nothing for the morale of the invasion forces. They were ready, the adrenaline was flowing, and keeping them penned up on invasion craft was devastating. Accordingly, although weather forecasts were still not good, the decision was made to go on June 6, and we were notified immediately.

Since we could not predict how strong the resistance from the Luftwaffe would be, it had

The most popular Canadian wing commander was undoubtedly Lloyd V. Chadburn, DSO and Bar, DFC, Croix de Guerre, seen here with his personal Spitfire V, coded with his initials, LVC, EP 548. Note the later exhaust style.

— courtesy Chadburn family

been decided to keep the strongest possible team of pilots together for the occasion. Pilots who had been near the end of their operational tour had been held back, and we had the strongest team from the point of experience that we had ever had. "Chad" Chadburn was the Winco, Bob Buckham was our CO in 403 Squadron, and I believe Johnny McElroy led 416, and Bill Prest 421.

We were advised that our wing would be flying patrols over the beachhead at 1,500 feet, and our sole job was to protect the landing groups from attack by enemy aircraft. We were to do our assigned job, and that job only, unless called upon by the controller to carry out some other task. We would do four one-hour patrols over the beachhead starting at 8:00 A.M., then 12:00 P.M., 4:00 P.M., and 8:00 P.M. Our teams were made up, and I found I'd be on the 12:00 P.M. and 8:00 P.M. shows.

I doubt that many of us would have gotten any sleep anyway, but any thought of sleep was made impossible by the steady stream of multi-engined aircraft that began parading across the south of England heading for France. We learned later that these were bombers, paratroop transports, and others pulling big Horsa gliders carrying troops and equipment. The "big show" had begun!

W/C Lloyd V. Chadburn with his personal Spitfire IX, LVC, ML 580, in May 1944. — courtesy Chadburn family

James Douglas Lindsay, from Arnprior, Ontario, in the cockpit of his Spitfire IX on May 7, 1944. — courtesy J.D. Lindsay

Previous Page: F/O Gord Ockenden in Spitfire IX, 2I-V, 443 Squadron.

AIR COMBAT

J. D. (Doug) Lindsay, 403 Squadron

D-DAY AND THE PERIOD immediately following was extremely hectic for fighter squadrons of Second TAF and has elsewhere been appropriately recorded by many historians.

However, from a *personal* point of view, not a great deal was happening, as our 403 Squadron, "City of Calgary," seemed to be engaged in many routine patrols with no contact of enemy aircraft. We seemed to always be in the air when the enemy was not, and on the ground when the Luftwaffe decided to put up a defensive effort. Consequently we had reports of other Spitfire squadrons doing battle with Me 109s and FW 190s and running up impressive scores. It seemed particularly galling that the other Canadian Spitfire squadrons were getting a lot of press about their exploits, when we got so little about our armed reconnaissance and front line patrols. As an example, on June 12, 1944, our sister squadron, 421, on 127 Wing, fought with thirty-plus Me 109s and FW 190s, and managed to destroy eleven of the enemy with the loss of only one aircraft, while occasionally we were called upon for missions in support of the ground troops, which seemed hardly appropriate for a keen Spitfire pilot who wanted to test his skills against enemy pilots.

There is no question that a test of machine against machine and flying skill against flying skill was the essence of every fighter pilot's dream. We knew the Spitfire's performance was as good as, if not better than the Me 109s or the FW 190s, so flying skills became the real competition. Strafing a truck convoy or a train, or bombing a road or rail bridge may well have contributed more to winning the war — but shooting down an enemy aircraft was decidedly the goal of every fighter pilot.

Thus the days immediately following D-day were particularly disappointing to me. Having had some limited success against enemy fighters prior to D-day, and having high expectations of a great deal of action on the part of the Luftwaffe to stem the invasion of Normandy, the inactivity

of our squadron was indeed a let down.

However, in the early morning of June 26, 1944, I was sitting "alert" with three other members of my flight when we were scrambled to intercept an incoming low-level attack. We were no sooner vectored by radar control to meet the attack when we found ourselves in the midst of at least twelve Me 109s at about 200 feet, heading towards our base. We immediately attacked, whereupon they broke formation and started to climb for the cloud base, which was at approximately 1,800 feet above ground level. I managed to get into firing position behind an enemy aircraft and had got off a few rounds, witnessing several strikes, when we were attacked by six or more long-nose FW 190s (the newest version for the FW 190). I called a break into the attack as the 190s made a firing pass and then climbed up into cloud to escape. We followed, hoping to make contact above cloud, but unfortunately that was the last we saw of them, so we returned to base and claimed one Me 109 damaged.

On the afternoon of June 29, 1944, I was leading Yellow Section on an armed recce in the Bernay-Liagle-Argentan area when radar reported enemy aircraft in our area. I immediately called for a maximum climb to 15,000 feet and upon breaking through a layer of cloud saw a formation of twelve-plus FW 190s at about our two o'clock position, approximately eight miles and slightly down sun. While manoeuvring the section to close up sun of the formation, they must have seen us, and broke formation and dove for the cloud layer which we had climbed through a few minutes prior. We gave chase, and as I broke out below cloud I saw an FW 190 firing on a Spitfire below and to my left. I called a "break left to Spitfire being attacked" (not knowing if he was even on the same radio transmitter channel I was broadcasting on), and immediately dove to attack the FW 190, which was still firing on the Spitfire. I opened up with all guns and got strikes on the

FW 190, which began shedding pieces and blew up. I turned my attention to the stricken Spitfire, and as I circled closer to examine the damage I noticed it was KH-E, one of our squadron aircraft. I saw the canopy release and the pilot exit the aircraft, which rolled over and dove into the ground. The parachute deployed, and the descending pilot drifted out of sight. On landing at home base I learned that the downed pilot was W/O Shannon. He had been flying with Blue Section on the same armed recce that we had started out on that afternoon. He returned to the squadron a week or so later, when the American ground forces overran the position where he had landed safely and hidden out behind enemy lines.

On July 3 we were scheduled to carry out a front line patrol at 8,000 feet flying three sections of four — each section following at approximately five minute intervals. I was flying ML 411, KH-K, and leading Yellow Section, S/Lt. E. P. Wood was leading Red Section and F/Lt. Andy MacKenzie was leading Blue Section. Shortly after reaching our patrol altitude Red and Blue Sections were advised that there were enemy aircraft approximately twenty miles west of their positions. I immediately called for a climb and headed our section due south. We topped the cloud deck at 19,000 feet, and I spotted a formation of fifteen or more Me 109s ahead of us, turning east. We immediately dropped our auxiliary fuel tanks and

gave chase. I fired on a straggling 109 at the 800 yard maximum range with a 20 mm cannon and got strikes on the aircraft. The pilot immediately ejected. The other aircraft started to turn left and descended through a large break in the cloud. We continued to overtake, and I opened up with all guns when another 109 came into range on my gyro gun sight. I observed several strikes on his aircraft, and when he tried to make a sharp evasive manoeuvre his right wing collapsed and the aircraft started to tumble. Meanwhile, we could hear both Red and Blue Sections also involved in a battle with twenty-plus Me 109s somewhere below us.

Suddenly we were enveloped in a melee of fighters — enemy and friendly — diving and turning, all firing their guns at each other. The picture of what an aerial dogfight might look like.

I managed to get on the tail of another Me 109 and when in range, opened up and continued firing until his aircraft blew up.

I then looked around for another enemy to attack, when I realized that the radio chatter had ceased, and the sky appeared to be empty. I was alone. Just as quickly as the fight had started, it was over.

We had tangled with more than thirty-five enemy fighters and destroyed six, probably destroyed one, and damaged five others, without a single loss.

I recall thinking how incredible it was that twelve of us in Spitfires could engage in aerial combat with a larger force of enemy fighters, without as much as a second thought about taking them on. What remarkable confidence we had in our aircraft. What a remarkable aircraft — the Spitfire.

Opposite: Members of the 403 Wolf Fighter Squadron in August 1943. Front row: F/O Joseph P. Lecoq, Montreal; F/L Charles P. Thornton, Detroit; P/O John Allen Wilson, Hamilton; Sgt. Stanley Barnes, Toronto; F/O Stanley W. Matthews, Winnipeg; W/O1 Clinton F. Rae, Moulinette, Ont.; and Sgt. James R. MacKinnon, Winnipeg. Middle row:F/O Livingston Foster, Grimsby, Ont.; F/O Robert G. Middlemiss, Montreal; F/O James F. Lambert, Winnipeg; F/L Dean Dover, Mount Dennis, Toronto; S/L Frank E. (Bitsy) Grant, Brockville, Ont.; W/C J.E. Johnson, DSO and bar, DFC and bar; F/L Noel J. Ogilvie, Ottawa; F/O Harry Dowding, Sarnia, Ontario; F/O J.D. Browne, Florham Park, New Jersey; P/O Paul K. Gray, Toronto. Back row: F/O Thomas A. Brannagan, Windsor, Ont.; F/O John Hodgson, Calgary; F/L Arthur C. Coles, North Vancouver, BC; F/L Herbert J. Southwood, Calgary; Sgt. Norman V. Chevers, Niagara Falls, Ont.;F/O James Preston, St. Catharines, Ont.; F/L David Goldberg, Hamilton; F/O Malcolm J. Gordon, Edmonton; and F/L Harry A. Pattinson, Hamilton.

— RCAF official photo PL 19718

MY MOST MEMORABLE EXPERIENCE

Norm Chevers, 403 and 132 Squadrons

I FLEW THE SPITFIRE IN 403 SQUADRON RCAF. It was considered one of the top squadrons in the air force. Many of the pilots had been flying instructors in Canada, had a lot of experience, and had already logged many hours of flying time.

I flew with W/C Johnnie Johnson, the top British ace, and I am shown in one of the group pictures with the squadron. We had the early Mark IXs, which were a big improvement over the Mark Vs.

My most memorable experience was on July 3, 1944, not long after D-day. I had been moved to 132 Squadron RAF, and was flying a Spitfire IX B, coded FF-K (serial NH 189) along with my number two, on an armed recce over enemy territory. We were slated on these missions to shoot-up any enemy military rolling stock. It so happened that we spotted some trucks on a road, away from any built-up areas.

I told number two we were going down. On a low-level attack, if you are pressing for good strikes, you are obligated to get quite close.

On the way down I held fire on my cannons until I was below 200 feet. Needless to say at this height and that close, you are pretty sure of making a hit. As I pressed the trigger for the cannons, I noticed a large explosion from the truck in front of me. I was too close to take an evasive action, and flew into the explosion. My number two thought I had crashed. After going into the ball of fire, I pulled up into a climbing turn to the left.

The Spit suffered a fair amount of damage, but I was OK. After testing and checking for damage, the oil pressure started dropping, so I knew I had taken some damage in the oil tank. We decided to go as far as we could in trying to bring the aircraft back.

After about five minutes, heading for friendly territory, I also noticed the temperature on the coolant had started to rise. I realized I wasn't going to make it to my own airfield, so I elected to land at a forward base. In this case it was B-6, just inside our own lines.

By this time the temperature had reached a very dangerous level, and I had to land quickly. On my final approach I shut the switches on the engine off and dead-sticked in for a landing. I expected the engine to blow up any second, and after touching down and braking heavily I proceeded to slide the hood back and open the cockpit door. Before the craft stopped rolling, I had jumped out and was running across the runway away from the Spit.

A few seconds later I heard a whistle. I turned around, and the fire crew were at the aircraft. They were waving at me to come back. They wanted to show me what had happened.

Then I checked the aircraft for damage. The right aileron was slashed its entire length, there was a lot of damage to the right wing and to a hold under the front of the fuselage, where the oil tank is attached to the engine.

In fact, there wasn't any oil left, and I had flown the aircraft for about eight minutes without oil. It was a good indication that the makers of the motor and airframe did an excellent job of manufacturing. The aircraft had to be written off for any future operations.

On July 5, I went to England for a new kite. It was a new Mark IX E (NH 465), with wing cannon and fifty calibre machine guns and wing bomb racks. It became FF-K as well. On July 8, 1944, on a beachhead patrol, in FF-K, I ran into some FW 190s. I destroyed one, and received congratulations all around. Included was Sir Archibald Sinclair, the British Air Minister, who thanked Canadian fighter pilots for the "glorious service" they were giving!

Opposite: Norm Chevers of Niagara Falls with his RAF Spitfire, FF-K, NH 189, displaying the 132 Squadron's "City of Bombay" crest, July 3, 1944. — RCAF official photo PL 29335

A Great Way to Start a New Job

W. R. "Bill" McRae

On July 26, 1944, 401 squadron was out on an armed reconnaissance of the area to the south and east of Paris. Returning home we were subjected to heavy flak from the German base at Dreux, shooting down our S/Lt. Hap Kennedy. Later that day Charlie Trainor, a flight commander in 411 Squadron, was promoted to squadron leader of 401.

At 6:00 A.M. the following morning, with Trainor leading us for the first time, we went looking for trouble in the Argentan region. We were flying at about 10,000 feet when I spotted a number of aircraft several thousand feet above us and a mile or two to the west, flying in our direction. From the ragged line abreast Trainor could not spot them, and he asked me to take over and lead him to them. I was flying Yellow Three, so with my wingman I pulled ahead and started climbing. Trainor soon picked up the Jerries and took over again. We could now see there were fifteen of them, mostly 109s but at least one 190. As we climbed we curved in behind, until, at about 15,000 feet, we were flying virtually in line astern with them. Incredibly, they still had not seen us. At about 300 yards Trainor called, "Every man for himself," or words to that effect, and opened fire.

The 109 I was moving in on was carrying a long-range tank, indicating that they had not yet been engaged. He dropped the tank and broke hard to the left, leaving vapour trails from his wingtips. I had no trouble turning inside him, but could not lead him enough for a shot without losing sight of him beneath the nose. We went around like this a couple of times, then he suddenly straightened out and closed his throttle. I rolled out of the turn with him and closed my throttle. For a fleeting moment I had a perfect target fifty yards straight ahead of me, but the Spitfire decelerated more slowly than the 109, and I was still overtaking him. My first concern was to avoid a collision, but I couldn't turn away without losing sight of him. Ramming on full rudder I skidded out to the right, preventing a roll with the ailerons. This got me clear of his tail, but I was still going to slide past. By aggressively fishtailing I managed to get slowed down to his speed, and for a few moments we were literally flying in formation, near the stall, wingtips nearly touching, while we stared at each other across the thirty-odd feet between us. Then he opened the throttle, momentarily leaving me behind. I soon caught up, and to avoid a repeat performance, opened fire from about 300 yards. Immediately something detached, and as it came sailing past my left wingtip I could see it was his canopy. I fired again, and this time he bailed out. As he too flashed by my wing I could see his parachute beginning to open.

Immediately I turned steeply to the left, both to check my rear and to keep the chute in sight. The sky was empty. It never failed to amaze me the way the sky could be full of aircraft one minute and empty the next. I was determined to get credit for this guy, but this time there was no wingman to corroborate, and since my guns were not firing at the moment he bailed out there would be no camera evidence. I decided, foolishly perhaps, that I would photograph the parachute. Using the camera gun only I flew directly at him until the parachute filled my windscreen and another second would have ended in collision. Satisfied, I checked my instrument panel for the first time and was shocked to see I was at 3,000 feet. This was no place to be when crossing the lines near Caen, so I climbed out of light flak range and set course for home, with a good deal of looking over my shoulder.

When we tallied up the score later it was seven 109s, one 190, and no losses. Eight pilots had shot down one each. This was probably 401s best single trip score to date — certainly during my tour with the squadron. My number two claimed he saw the Jerry bail out and his chute open. But since my number two was nowhere to be seen when I circled the parachute I assumed that he had seen someone else's victim. In any case I got a good picture of the parachute and there was no argument about the claim. A great way to start the day, and a great way for Charlie Trainor to start his new job.

Spitfire IX, NH 243, 411 Squadron, Digby, England. — courtesy Clerihew

Spitfire IX, DN-B, BS 319, of 416 Squadron, showing wing shape and camouflage.

— National Archives of Canada PA 136898

MOURNFUL

W. R. "Bill" McRae

ALMOST EVERYONE HAD A NICKNAME, some less flattering than others. It was Arthur Bishop who bestowed on me the name "Mournful," deservedly, during the winter of 1943–44. A dour Scot by nature, at this time I was feeling particularly low and it showed, making me a natural for tagging with the name of that "L'il Abner" comic strip character, Mournful Bagley. Now I can tell "Bish" why.

Perhaps I had read too many World War I stories as a boy, and had preconceived ideas about what to expect as a fighter pilot. I left Spitfire OTU early in July 1941, full of expectations about life on an operational squadron, only to discover that luck, fate, or just the odds would play a big part in my future. I believe it was Stanford Tuck who said that "luck is half the battle," but I soon concluded I'd need luck to be *in* a battle.

I had gone overseas in a small freighter with three others from my course, Jack Milmine, Bill Wallace and Wally McLeod. Wally went to a different OTU, and then presumably directly to an active squadron in 11 Group, where the action was, as had most of the others from my graduating class at Camp Borden. Milmine was killed at our OTU. On graduation Bill Wallace and I were posted to 132, a newly forming RAF squadron in Scotland. During the winter of 1941–42 we had a flight (not mine) seconded to Sumburgh on the Shetlands, from which point they were escorting Hudsons to Norway, with Spitfire II Bs, *without drop tanks*. They had fuel for eight minutes over the target, and prayed they would not be engaged since, had they been, the chances of getting home were virtually nil. During my eleven months with this unit we lost half a dozen pilots, including Bill Wallace, all but one due to operational accidents while flying scrambles and patrols in atrocious weather. During this time we had seen just one German aircraft, a hit-and-run Ju 88 which bombed our field; not one of us had had the opportunity to fire our guns at anything but a target.

In May of 1942 I was posted to the Middle East, and I believed my fortune would change when I reached the Desert Air Force. Fate, however, was to intervene once again. En route to Cairo I was diverted and ended up in an operational unit in a backwater location on the Gold Coast, where the prospects of shooting at anything were extremely remote. When I arrived back in England in May 1943, I had been overseas two years, had logged about 500 hours on Spitfires and Hurricanes, but had never fired my guns in anger. I considered a fighter pilot's role was to shoot down enemy aircraft, and this goal seemed destined to elude me. The stigma of being a scoreless fighter pilot had brought me close to depression by the end of my tenure in Africa, but once again I felt my luck was about to change.

On learning that I was earmarked for Typhoons, on which I could envisage never having an opportunity to shoot down anything, I went to RCAF Headquarters in London and wangled a posting to 401 Squadron, then on rest at Catterick, Yorkshire. On June 1 we moved to Redhill, Surrey, to become part of 126 Airfield, later 126 Wing. I was now in the right theatre of war, at a good time, but once again the odds were against me. The wings of our Mark V Spits were clipped, the superchargers cropped, and for the next six months we were relegated almost exclusively to low-level close escort duty to Venturas, Bostons, Mitchells, and Marauders, attacking mainly German airfields in France and Belgium. Although 401 would eventually become the highest scoring Canadian Spitfire squadron, during this period we rarely saw a Jerry aircraft, but fumed while we listened to the radio chatter of the high cover, Johnnie Johnson's Canadian wing from Kenley, who were engaged — and scoring — on nearly every raid.

By November of 1943 we had been equipped with Mark IXs. We still continued to fly escort, but more frequently the top cover. Alas, the Jerries who had been there for the Kenley boys were now home in Germany, defending against the United States Eighth Air Force, and once again we were flying in empty skies — except for the omnipresent flak. We had some measure of success in flying four- and eight-man rangers, mini-sweeps trying to catch Jerry bombers moving up each evening for the mini-blitz of London.

Even now, the odds seemed against me. I was out on a sweep over northern France one morning, where we encountered nothing. Then the afternoon shift went out to the same area and came across six FW 190s circling a field, waiting for a crashed Me 410 to be moved off the runway. They were so engrossed in watching the recovery progress that they had no idea 401 had joined the party, until four of their number were burning on the ground, the other two and the crashed 410 damaged. Luck!

One week before D-day there was a sign that not all my luck was bad. We were about to take off for a sweep of the Normandy area. My aircraft was unserviceable, so I had been assigned another. My number two for the day, Cy Cohen, came over to me and said the aircraft I was using was usually his, could we exchange? It made no difference to me so we changed places. About mid-Channel on the way home Cy's engine quit, and he bailed out too low. It gave me a spooky feeling looking down at the green dye where he had gone in but failed to come up. There but for *chance* go I.

The imminence of the Invasion was obvious to anyone flying over southern England, and I was desperate to be in on it. I was becoming paranoid at the thought of going home and, on being asked, "How many did you shoot down," having to admit that I had not even shot *at* any! By the time we moved into France to stay on June 22 I had seen the demise of at least twenty assorted Jerry aircraft, but had yet to fire my guns at one. I had done my share of shooting up ground transports, and dropping bombs, but to me this did not count. Without having experienced the situation it is impossible to understand my frustration, almost shame, at my scoreless record.

Then finally, on the second of two four-man patrols I led out of Beny sur Mer on the morning of July 7, flying my regular aircraft MK 560, YO-L, the jinx was broken. We had completed our shift and were returning to base, flying at 5,000 feet with the ceiling 500 feet above us. Suddenly a dozen or so Me 109s flying in ragged line abreast popped out of the clouds almost over our heads, flying in the opposite direction. A quick look around showed that they had not seen us, because they continued on. As I was turning my section around to pursue, I called base to scramble four more, having a gut feeling that this formation was not alone. We had no trouble catching up, coming up behind and slightly below until we were within 300 yards, when I told my guys to pick a target, each for himself. At that point we were spotted, and the Jerries all broke to the left. I turned into the one directly ahead of me, and with a large deflection angle fired a three second burst (according to the camera gun record). I could see cannon strikes in the wing root and fuselage side, ahead of the cockpit, but he kept going. A second burst gave strikes in the cockpit as well as the wing root; pieces were shed and a short streak of flame came from the wing. He flicked out of the steep left bank into a right-hand spin, from which Tony Williams and Art Bishop, my number three and four, confirmed he did not recover, crashing near Lisieux. I now had a second one in my sights and fired just as he disappeared into cloud. I climbed through, as it was only 500 feet thick, but they wisely remained hidden and escaped. Meanwhile, my gut feeling had been correct; the second four scrambled ran into about twenty-five mixed 190s and 109s, also in the Lisieux area, getting one before they too took cover in the cloud.

It was only three weeks short of three years since I had joined my first squadron. Strangely, I felt no elation for this first victory, only a profound sense of relief that the drought was over. When I viewed the camera gun photos later they showed a 109 at close range at a large angle of bank, but the cannon strikes that I had clearly seen were not evident on the film. Had Bishop not confirmed the kill it is quite likely my claim would have been denied, which would have been the cruelest twist of fate and the final irony of my career. So, Bish, you are forgiven for the Mournful tag!

RWM

W. R. "Bill" McRae

THE WINTER OF 1943–44 WAS VERY COLD, and often in the early mornings at Biggin Hill we would have heavy frost to clear off our wings and the windshield to defrost before we could start out. The Spitfire's snug cockpit was not suited to the bulky coveralls we had worn during winter flying in Canada, and it became very uncomfortable for us flying at 25,000 feet in just battle dress. This was overcome by issuing us with two-piece electrically heated overalls. I, and I think most fellows, found the trouser half too restrictive, and so did not use them. But the top was loose enough to be quite comfortable. It was worn over our battle dress, and having no rank markings, served to make everyone of equal rank to the casual observer. We used this feature often when away from base to take our non-commissioned pilots with us into the officers' mess, a small demonstration of our disapproval of this unfortunate rank discrimination.

Our wing commander at this time was Buck McNair. Toward the end of February, Buck came over to me saying he would be away for a short time, during which I would be responsible for his aircraft, adding, "Whatever you do, don't bend it!" I have no idea why he picked me. Over the next ten days I flew McNair's aircraft, with his personal RWM markings, on six operations, plus a number of training flights. Returning from some of the sorties we were low on fuel, landing as we often did at Manston to refuel before going on to Biggin Hill. When we taxied in, I, in RWM bearing the wing commander's pennant and my electric jacket hiding the fact I was a lowly F/Lt., would get priority service from the local crews. I was helped down from the wing, refuelled first, my perspex polished. There was some good natured grumbling from my peers about Mac getting this kind of attention while the rest in YO aircraft had to take their turn.

Sgt. Pilot O.F. Pickell of 412 Squadron in Spitfire V, "Thunderbird II," VZ-T, AD 318, in October or November 1941.
It was the first to be delivered with a "negative G" carburetor.

DIVE BOMBER

Tommy Koch, 401 Squadron

THE SPITFIRE WAS TO FULFILL many roles during the war. One aspect was the dive-bomber missions it was called on to perform, especially in 1944. Thus, our aircraft in 401 Squadron were equipped in 1944 to carry a 250-pound bomb under each wing, and a 500-pound bomb under the fuselage. Targets were "no ball" (buzz bomb launchers), oil tanks, railway lines and bridges.

Accuracy was not of the highest calibre, but it added excitement to our job. I do recall leaving oil tanks blazing, hitting a railway line — hopefully delaying delivery of goods, and a good concentration on a bridge. What I found exciting was flying through the flak on the dive. The flak would be coming up and passing by the aircraft, and after dropping the bombs and pulling up, the flak would be coming up and surrounding the aircraft as it climbed away.

As a point of interest, it was decided that we could carry a 1,000-pound bomb if tests proved satisfactory. These bombs were to be test-dropped into the Channel, and if all went well, we would be using them on occasion. One Spitfire was equipped with just such a bombload, much to the unhappy pilot's dismay, as there was very little clearance between the bomb and the runway when the pilot taxied out. However the first two bombs carried by the pilots released properly, and the aircraft came back for its third bomb drop.

When the pilot of this third drop made the attempt to drop, the bomb hung up, and on the

Tommy Koch

pull-out from the dive, the bomb pulled out part of the bottom of the fuselage. The aircraft returned to base alright, but much to our relief that put an end to the proposed 1,000-pound bomb on Spitfires.

A wet day in 1944 with 401 Squadron at DeRips.

WAS IT ROMMEL?

W. R. "Bill" Weeks, 442 Squadron

I HAVE APPENDED BELOW A TALE not previously committed to paper, nor related to any but my own immediate family. It is for your files, those cardboard folders, or that circular one which is most often conveniently placed near to one's desk. Take your pick!

During the early evening of July 17, 1944, in Spitfire MK 416, Y2-D, while flying wingman to Louis Cochand, I sighted a German staff car, along with its motorcycle escort, proceeding west along the Villers Bocage–Caen Highway. I put my aircraft into a steep dive, levelled out at a height of about 300 feet, and fired a short burst.

In rapid succession I observed the following: the driver collapsed over the steering wheel, the car came to an instantaneous stop, and a general either jumped, or was thrown from the vehicle. Since his exit was on the far side of the car from me, I could not see whether or not he was injured.

When I pulled up after the attack, I could see, in the gathering twilight, Louis' aircraft circling over the hills to the southwest of Caen.

Our flight path on the way back to our base at Beny sur Mer took us over a German flak belt. The 40 mm projectiles, which looked like yellow tennis balls, seemed to rise gently toward us; when they neared our aircraft, they appeared to accelerate rapidly, and to crisscross 'round and about our aircraft.

Louis, not an imprudent man, seemed to be enjoying the fireworks. I, to put it mildly, would have preferred more altitude. For some considerable time after the attack, I kept wondering why the car came to such an abrupt halt. I was not to know until later.

Approximately a week later, B. E. Middleton, also of 442 Squadron, and an excellent pilot, said to me, "That general you got last week had to be Rommel." I explained to "Bo" (the only name he ever used) that since Rommell was reportedly injured on July 19, and I had not flown that day, it must have been some other high-ranking officer. As he walked away from me, Bo turned and said, "Don't be too sure of that, I still think it was Rommel."

Not being convinced, I more or less dismissed the incident from my mind. However, in May 1954 my wife, June, gave me a copy of Chester Wilmot's book, *The Struggle for Europe*. His account of the incident is so vivid and consistent with what I have written here that I am no longer in doubt.

I had been intending for a long time to write to B. E. Middleton and tell him that he was without doubt right! Alas, I learned in October 1991 from my former number two, Al Bathurst, that Bo had recently passed away.

LAC Charlie Thompson adjusts the camera of 414 Squadron Spitfire MJ 615, A/C "B".

PHOTO RECONNAISSANCE

Harry Furniss, 400 Squadron RCAF

THE SPITFIRE WAS THE SUPREME fighter aircraft of World War II. It has been lovingly and accurately described as erotically responsive and tender to fly, deadly in combat, and the most beautiful fighter ever built.

Special Spitfires were developed for photo reconnaissance. The Mark XI version, which equipped 400 Squadron, RCAF, in the latter part of the war, carried no armament, no armour plate protection, just cameras — thirty-six inch focal plane verticals with automatic timing controls for precision line-overlaps and mosaics.

Camouflaged in pale blue paint, this aircraft was virtually invisible at 30,000 feet, operational height. Extra fuel tanks gave us a range of about 1,500 miles — London–Berlin return with a good reserve. This could be increased with drop tanks to allow up to seven hours flying. Normal cruising speed was 320 TAS at high altitude, and maximum speed was 420 at 25,000 feet.

All the technical data in the world does little to describe the absolute thrill of flying a Spitfire. No matter what your experience, the fantastic high as you poured the boost to the mighty Merlin engine stayed long after the flight. The Spit just had it all — superb handling characteristics and feather-light manoeuvrability, effortless aerobatics — climbing rolls after takeoff, and an engine that purred with incredible power and reliability.

It was with 400 Squadron and their pale-blue unarmed Spitfires that I served the longest. Life in a photo recce squadron lacked the blood bonding of other fighting units — the morale-sustaining teamwork of a heavy bomber crew or the visible support of fighter pilots, who seldom flew in groups of less than six. The solitary role of the spyplane in hostile skies called for an unusual personality. In choosing the pilots for 400 Squadron, some unknown personnel genius had dealt a perfect hand. Each of us was a certifiable loner, a self-sufficient operator with superior flying skills who could observe, record and understand what the war was all about. This bouillabaisse of personalities and temperaments was uniquely suited to the bloody lonely, tough and dangerous work of unarmed reconnaissance of the enemy.

My first solo operational sortie quickly introduced me to the special hazards of recce work. The sky was thick with dirty grey clouds as I gently lifted my Spitfire off the runway at Odiham, England, and headed for the continent of Europe. It was May 24, 1944, in Spitfire XI serial PA 829.

From 2,000 feet through to 15,000 feet I could see nothing but the instrument panel in front of my nose, and the occasional glimpse of a wingtip. Moisture streamed off the windscreen, but there were no signs of icing. There was little turbulence, which gave me hope that there weren't any dangerous cumulonimbus thunderheads imbedded in this muck.

I reached 30,000 feet, operational level, in relative clear, but the thick blanket below blotted out the whole world. I checked the time; I should be over the first line of flak batteries on the French coast. With a touch of bravado, I changed course erratically to throw off their radar-directed fire.

But I saw nothing. Ten minutes later I was almost over the target area. I felt it was foolish to carry on, and I told myself I couldn't take pictures through this, so I turned for home.

Ten minutes later I was talking to myself again. I couldn't go home without checking out the target area, or I'd be letting the whole side down. I turned back on course, and ten minutes later I was within thirty miles of the target area. I could see that it was still hopeless, and pictures were impossible, and turned once more for home. After five more minutes I said to myself, Furniss, just because nobody's watching you doesn't mean you can go home yet. The cloud cover looked thinner. Maybe I should go down and check the ceiling. I turned back on course, and started down.

In another ten minutes I was down to 5,000 feet, in dense cloud. I went down 2,000 more, but no breaks or thinning. I daren't go any lower without a fix on my position. I was well into the target area, and there's no way I could take pictures. I turned for home with a clear conscience.

When I reckoned I was safely over the Channel on the way home, I let down cautiously and broke into the clear over water at 2,000 feet. When the English coast didn't appear on time, I switched on the radio and asked for a check on my position. The answer came back quickly, "Continue present course — 265 degrees."

After ten minutes, and still no land in sight, I thought I should give it another ten minutes. But there was still no land, and twenty minutes flying at 300 mph is one hundred miles. Where's the bloody coast? Fuel still OK, but it's time to start worrying.

I called control again for a check on position. A different cool English voice told me to steer 025 degrees. What the heck — why was I doing a right-hand turn in the middle of the Channel? The controller confirmed the course, so I decided to give it ten minutes. Twenty minutes later, I landed safely at home, and the intelligence officer explained it all.

The Germans continuously monitored our radio frequencies. When conditions were right, they passed out false radar homings. This was a popular trick in the wide open sky, and quite successful with us new boys.

I must have drifted considerably southwards during my time above the clouds. My course home, instead of taking me across the narrow Strait of Dover towards London, was taking me parallel to the south coast, out the Channel towards the open Atlantic Ocean. No wonder the German controller (probably near Brussels, and close to my original call) was so quick to confirm it as correct! By the time I asked for the second homing, I was out of his range and back into my own. Makes your neck-hairs tingle!

Later on the Germans introduced their V-2 rocket. It was potentially more deadly than the V-1 buzz bombs they had already been launching. It arrived silently at supersonic speed. There was no defence. It was launched vertically by mobile ground equipment, had a range of 200 miles, and flew through the sound barrier on a high inverted V-shaped trajectory guided by radio.

By chance, on September 16, 1944, in Spitfire PL 826, I spotted one of the first V-2 launchings, and took some photos of the site and equipment. I was returning across France from a photo recce job, when suddenly this strange contrail zipped by vertically off my wingtip. Sighting back down this arrow of white, I estimated the point on the ground where the object had originated, and turned the cameras on.

Soon, word came back of a huge explosion in London at the same time I had been taking my pictures. Sure enough, one of my photos revealed some V-2 transport and launching equipment. They would go on to kill at least 3,000 people before the war ended, besides messing up acres of urban real estate.

After that, I went to 401 Squadron, flying Spitfire IX fighter aircraft. One of my aircraft, MJ 271, YO-D, ended up in a museum in Holland. Then I was shot down by an FW 190 while I was flying EN 549, YO-Y, on March 1, 1945, so my fighter career was rather brief.

Note the camera bulge to the side of the roundel on the fuselage of 430 Squadron Spitfire XIV, RM 817.

— courtesy 430 Squadron groundcrew

PHOTO RECONNAISSANCE

Mike Carr, 414 Squadron

I TOOK MY FIRST AIRPLANE RIDE AS A BOY in my home town of Ingersoll, Ontario, at a little airshow. The ride cost me a dollar. We went up and turned around and landed. I didn't like that much, as I wanted to do more. I hardly dreamed then that I would be flying as a pilot myself in such a wonderful plane as the Spitfire.

I already had about 1,000 hours in the RCAF, including time spent instructing. So I had my choice of what I wanted to do, and chose single-engine fighters.

I joined 414 Squadron, and flew Mustangs, and then Spitfires. I used to fly number two to our CO, Gord Wonnacott, a terrific guy. It was a photo reconnaissance squadron, but we were also armed. Our Spitfires carried 20 mm cannons, but we were supposed to fire them only in self-defence. We did fire them once in a while on targets, including tanks and trains.

On one sortie I was on, there was a battalion-size unit of Germans marching along a road. I could see an officer on a white horse, and about

Mike Carr and his 414 Squadron Spitfire IX, MJ 518, aircraft "O" in 1944. — courtesy Mike Carr

A group shot of 414 Fighter-Recon Squadron at B-21 airbase in France, 1944. — courtesy Mike Carr

ninety soldiers behind him. We decided to strafe the road. I made sure I flew clear of my wingman as we came down, and I flew down one side of the road, and my buddy flew alongside me, and we demolished that column.

That was the exception, as mainly we were detailed to find and select targets for the bombers or the Typhoons to take care of. As I have mentioned, we usually flew in pairs only, not as a squadron. I did love flying low, and in a photo squadron I had every excuse in the world to do it. We'd have to pull up over the hedgerows that were everywhere — up about three feet to clear them, and then back down again.

In a photo squadron, you had to fly perfectly straight to take pictures. Our main enemy was flak, but whether it was coming at you or not, you had to go through it to keep the film running. They set the cameras for a certain speed, around 260 mph. We followed our maps, strapped to our knees, and used the compass in our aircraft. You had to be a good navigator in a single-engined plane, especially doing our job of photography.

I had my wife's name, Helen, on my aircraft. When I crashed that plane, due to flak damage, I had *Helen II* on my new aircraft, coded 0, serial MJ 518. That is the aircraft I am having my picture taken with in October 1944.

I came home Christmas Eve, 1944. I was glad to see my wife after being away three and one-half years. I heard that the Luftwaffe made a big raid on our base right after that on New Year's day. One of our fellows, Bill Sayer, managed to get up, and shot down five of the raiders. It was the first time he had fired his guns in anger, and he won an immediate DFC before his tires even stopped rolling on the runway. I would have loved to have been there!

I never had a bad moment while flying the Spitfire, and enjoyed my time with 414, and the many friends I made. We had the best aircraft for the job, as the Mustangs seemed a bit heavy for the low altitude work. You couldn't beat the Spitfire — my favourite aircraft.

Mike Carr and his 414 Squadron Spitfire FR IX, "Helen II," MJ 518.

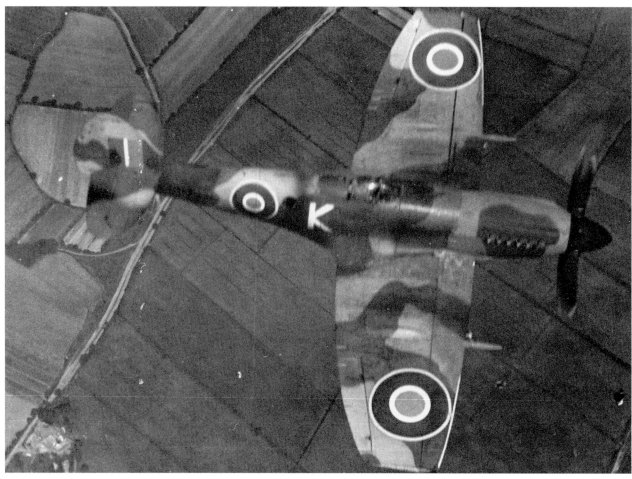

An aerial view of a 414 Squadron Spitfire XIV. — courtesy Dave McBride

Spitfire XI of 400 Squadron at its flooded base in Holland, 1945. Art Bowman is seen above the prop.

— DND PL 42675 courtesy Steve Sauvé

LAZY LADY

James B. Prendergast, 430 and 414 Squadrons

I COMMENCED FLYING MUSTANGS at OTU Howarden in November 1943. The Mustang I A we flew had a 1,200 hp Allison engine, with six, thirty calibre machine guns as armament, and three camera mounts. The supercharger was de-rated (cropped) to give more power at low level — up to 400 mph on the deck.

The Mustang was very comfortable to fly, easy to control with trim tabs. This was a "lazy lady," and so was the Spitfire.

We converted from Mustangs to Spitfire XIVs in November 1944. The Spitfire XIV FR we flew was far more powerful, with a 2,100 hp Rolls Royce Griffon engine, with a five blade prop. The FR (fighter reconnaissance) version we flew had two 20 mm cannons, four, fifty calibre machine guns, and four camera mountings for the photo work we did.

Reconnaissance squadrons did not normally have the three-letter battle letters, therefore senior pilots usually painted their initial on the aircraft, and could name their own aircraft — in my case *P* for Prendergast.

I had in all five lazy ladies. Two Mustangs and one Spitfire I lost through enemy flak. I also lost one Spitfire from enemy aircraft during the Luftwaffe attack on January 1, 1945, at Eindhoven, when I was trapped on the taxi path by other Spitfires ahead of me waiting to take off, and had to abandon mine before it was shot up. So all my aircraft were category Bs, and many were write-offs.

In this period, 430 squadron was based at B-78, Eindhoven, as part of 39R (reconnaissance) Wing, as part of Second Tactical Air Force.

C/O James B. Prendergast of 414 Squadron with his Spitfire XIV, "Lazy Lady IV," NH648.

G/C Bill MacBrien's old Spit V, used mainly for running errands and for urgent communication work, in 1944

A rare photo of Blair Dal Russel's Spitfire IX, BDR, ML 422, in September 1944. — courtesy Knutson

BUSTING THE AMMO TRAIN

Bill Weeks, 442 Squadron

DURING THE LATE FORENOON OF OCTOBER 15, a flight of four aircraft, with Don Goodwin leading and me leading the second section, took off from our new base at Voeghel, and dive-bombed a bridge on the outskirts of Utrecht. Goodwin then led us in a general direction toward Arnhem. We paralleled the rail line between Utrecht and Appledorn at a distance of about five miles to starboard. Roughly halfway between Utrecht and Appledorn, I spotted a large train parked outside a small town. I informed Don and told him that I was going to attack with my section. He said, "Go ahead, my section will cover you."

At a distance of five miles from the train, we were able to make a nice flat high speed attack. We succeeded in blowing the boilers of both locomotives pulling the train. After pulling up to about 400 feet, we did a slow 360-degree turn and attacked the first two cars behind the engines. When we again pulled up we could see flames and exploding ammunition. Goodwin's section then attacked the two rearmost cars and produced the same result. Both sections then attacked the cars in the central section of the train and set them afire.

As we circled above, watching our handiwork, we could see adjacent cars being ignited. In a few minutes the entire train was a mess of flames and intermittent explosions. At two o'clock that afternoon, a photo recce aircraft reported that the train was still burning. On the way back to base, we shot up another locomotive and destroyed five transports.

A 417 Squadron Spitfire VIII in Italy. — RCAF official photo PL 18757

The pilot (MacDonald?) tells Wyman, a member of the groundcrew, about a mission. This aircraft is Bill MacKenzie's 441 Squadron Spitfire IX, 9G-M, MK 417, in D-Day stripes, June 1944.

Wilf Banks with VZ-S in 1944. — courtesy Wilf Banks

A Brief Story

Wilf Banks, 412 Squadron

On December 5, 1944, I was stationed at an aerodrome at Vokel, in Holland. It was 10:55 A.M. when our section of five Spits took off for an armed reconnaissance. We quickly crossed over the front lines and into enemy territory. I was flying a Spit IX, ML 277. Ground control (Kenwood) called to warn us of enemy fighters in the area, and we engaged what looked like about fifty Me 109s, more or less. Anyway, it looked like a huge gaggle of what we called Huns. They started a left-hand turn, still in some sort of awkward formation, but as we attacked, the formation disintegrated into an every-man-for-himself format.

With throttle wide open I attacked a 109. He was unable to turn away from me, and I scored immediate strikes and he fell away streaming smoke and pieces. On looking around, I could see individual aircraft scattered all around the sky, but there was another 109 headed back to Germany, so with the throttle wide open I pursued him for about five minutes and got behind him. He saw me coming, but waited too long to turn, and he went the same way as the first one.

By this time, I had been engaged with different enemy aircraft at full throttle for about fifteen minutes. In an air battle involving this large a number of aircraft one looks for targets of opportunity. You make a quick pass if and when you get the chance, but you don't get locked in, or you will never see what hit you.

By now the sky was empty, and I was alone, not sure of where I was and not a friend or foe visible anywhere. I radioed Kenwood for a bearing home, got it, and set a compass course for base, knowing I had a long way to go. Within a few minutes, lo and behold, there, about 1,000 feet below and going the other way, was a lone Me 109 headed back to Germany. I half rolled, opened the throttle, and went after him. I had a distinct advantage, or so I thought, in that I was coming out of the sun. I also had the advantage of height and surprise, so it would be a victory quick and simple, or so I thought.

Not so, for he saw me immediately, and opened his throttle wide, the black smoke from his exhaust trailing behind. Just before I was in firing range, he broke just at the correct time, and I was unable to lay on sufficient deflection to open fire. The G-forces in the turn caused me to grey out, and I couldn't see until the stress of the turn was relieved. So I pulled away, regaining as much altitude as possible, and at the same time trying to see where he was.

From then on, we both jockeyed for position, and I attacked again with exactly the same thing happening as the first time. We went into this dogfight at about 7,000 feet, and when we were down to less than 1,000 feet, and after what seemed like fifteen minutes (it was probably only five), I decided to break it off, or risk an engine failure or running out of gas before getting home. We both seemed glad to go our separate ways. He went east, and I went west, with only a quick look back to make sure.

I landed back at base without further incident, and claimed two Me 109s destroyed. Our squadron claimed a total of four destroyed and one probable on that mission. We lost F/O C. W. Glithero, in MK 698, VZ-K, but I did not see what happened to him.

A 412 Squadron IX taxis past B-26 "La Paloma" of the USAAF, Heesch, on March 22, 1945.
— National Archives of Canada PA 115100

THE LAME FORTRESS

J. J. Boyle, 411 Squadron

A NOTATION IN MY LOGBOOK for February 24, 1945, simply states "escorted lame Fortress."

The day started with another dive-bombing sortie. We had all grown more than a little weary of attacking ground targets — not that we disliked strafing all that much, but we all hated dive-bombing. Our targets, such as bridges, rail lines or marshalling yards, were selected because of their strategic importance, and they were always well defended by anti-aircraft guns. It was very nerve-wracking to have to descend about 10,000 feet, almost vertically, into a hail of ack-ack fire — we could see the white-hot tracer fire coming at us from the moment it left the guns. Since we attacked in a single stream, one right after the other, it was most unnerving for the last guy, the "tail-end Charlie," for by the time he started his descent, the gunners had been able to correct their aim.

For six straight weeks without respite we had been assigned ground targets, and as a result squadron morale was low. As usual on our return to base, we went directly to operations to complete reports on the results of strikes. Imagine our delight to hear that a sweep was laid on for us that afternoon.

The purpose of a sweep was to sweep the skies clear of enemy fighters. We flew in full squadron strength and plotted our course, usually triangular, to cover all enemy airfields in our sector, hoping

John J. Boyle, DFC, with his 411 Squadron Spitfire "Winifred," DB-J, NH 471. Boyle was from Toronto and was one of Canada's ace pilots. — courtesy John Boyle

On Christmas 1944, J.J. "Jack" Boyle shot down a German jet Me 262 fighter-bomber while flying this aircraft, a Mark IX, DB-L, ML 686, seen in white above fin flash. As shown in this photo, soon after the sky band and spinner were painted over. DB-L was usually flown by Andy McNiece. Jack's usual aircraft, DB-R, RR 201, is pictured in the background. — courtesy Andy McNiece

to intercept and engage enemy fighter aircraft. Everyone was keen to be picked to fly a sweep because it seemed to us to be far more suitable for fighter pilots than the drudgery of dive-bombing. I was particularly pleased to see that I had been selected to lead the squadron. You could tell the other guys were pleased by this too, because just by the luck of the draw, whenever I led the squadron we seemed to find some action, and, touch wood, had never had a loss. Many of us were inclined to be superstitious and carried some sort of good luck charm. I had a pair of Sue's booties tied to my Mae West jacket. Spike Ireland, the other flight commander, always complained that he rarely enjoyed such luck whenever he led. However on this day it was my turn to have no luck, as we saw no enemy aircraft at all.

As we were just starting out on the first leg of our flight I could see a big gaggle of Flying Fortresses, B 17s, high above us, streaming long vapour trails and heading into Germany. They were the only aircraft we saw over the next hour, and we were all a little disappointed on our homeward leg. Unexpectedly, we came upon one lame Fort, with one prop feathered and one wheel hanging down, heading back in a westerly direction to his base in England. He had lost some 10,000 feet of altitude since I first saw him. Knowing it would be far better for him to land in Holland rather than risk the longer trip back to England, I decided to offer to help him, and told my second-in-command to take the squadron home.

There was a standard procedure for offering help to an aircraft in difficulty. I positioned myself several hundred yards to his left and flew on a parallel course. After showing him a plan view of my aircraft by flipping over on my side several times, I very gradually slid in closer to him until he could see my markings and know for sure I was friendly. Then I pulled in front of him and wiggled my wings back and forth. This said, "Follow me and I will lead you to safety." We were only about fifteen minutes away from Voekel Airfield, which I knew had paved runways long enough to accommodate the Fort. He lumbered along very slowly, and even though I had cut my throttle way back and had put down both my flaps and undercart to slow me up, my lead kept lengthening, and I had to keep circling back to pick up the slack every few minutes until Voekel came into sight.

In an effort to tell him he had problems with

his undercarriage, I lowered and raised my wheels several times until I could see his other wheel come down. Flying close underneath him, I could see no signs of damage, but I couldn't help wondering if it would all collapse the moment he touched down. Happily, he had no further problems and made a normal landing. By this time I was low on gas and decided to land as well. I pulled up to the visitors' hangar, and as I dismounted, the fort captain stood waiting for me. After introducing ourselves, during which time he kept pumping my hand in both of his, he told me their story.

He had a brand new crew, and this had been their first operational flight. He had completed one tour of operations and this was the first flight of his second tour. Shortly after I had first seen them on their way into Germany, he had been hit by high flak, but since damage had been slight, he had decided to stay with the main bombing force. Once over the target, he took a damaging hit that knocked out one engine, as well as his electrical, hydraulic, radio, and intercom systems. None of the crew had been injured. As they headed for home he couldn't keep up, and fell farther and farther behind. Two Mustangs, P 51s, stayed with

him as long as they could, but when they reached the end of their endurance, they had to abandon him too. Things were looking pretty desperate when we stumbled upon him. He didn't know exactly where he was, or if he had enough gas to get home, and was simply heading west hoping to see the English Channel any minute (when it was actually half an hour away).

While he was telling me this, his crew had gathered around us and were all listening intently, because this was news to them too. Without their intercom, many of them hadn't been at all sure what had happened over the last hour or so. He went on to say he couldn't believe their good luck when he sighted a squadron of Spitfires, and was profuse in his thanks for being down safe and sound. Just then the air gunner from the belly turret identified himself and said he owed me an apology. When he first saw me flipping my wings, he said, he had opened fire, not knowing if I were friend or foe. Thank God his aim had been just as bad as his aircraft recognition!

After gassing up I was back home in fifteen minutes, and although my report to operations would show no action with the enemy, it had been a very satisfying day.

"Winifred," DB-J, NH 471, of 411 Squadron. — courtesy Fochuk

RHUBARB

Michael Doyle, 411 Squadron

FEBRUARY 7, 1945, was not a very nice day. As I recall, it was a Sunday, at B-88, 126 Wing's airfield at Heesch, Holland. It was raining, and very cold. The sky was totally overcast, with the ceiling being probably around a couple of hundred feet, and most of the pilots on 411 Squadron had hunkered down in the mess or in the quarters for the day. In other words, not even the birds were flying.

I went over to the mess at about noon to get my lunch. The mess was in a shack- type building, and the food was never very great, but it was adequate. Before I could even sample the Sunday offering, however, J. J. (Jack Boyle) came over to me and said, "How about a rhubarb?" The previous day he and I and a couple of other pilots had done an armed recce into Germany, and on the way back we had passed over what looked like a temporary airstrip at Borkenberge, which appeared to be full of aircraft out in the open. At the time nobody in the flight had any ammo left, and we were short on fuel, so we carried on back to Heesch. But Jack had obviously not forgotten about it, and now he was looking for someone to accompany him to have a go at destroying those enemy aircraft. What could I say?

The two of us went down to the barn that served as our dispersal shack, and because Jack was a flight commander, he had no difficulty in arranging for a couple of Spitfires to be made ready to go. We got our gear, made out a sort of flight plan to get us to Borkenberge at ground level, and set out. He was flying his usual Spitfire RR 201, DB-R, *Sweet Sue V*, while I was in MK 788, DB-Z. The weather was still horrible! Also, I was not flying my usual aircraft, PK 992, DB-W.

En route, everything seemed to be just fine. We were flying right on the deck in fairly close formation, and every now and again Jack would give me a thumbs-up, which meant to me that we were on track for Borkenberge. In fact we were, and pretty soon Jack called over the VHF radio (we had maintained radio silence up to that point)

that our target was just ahead. I slid back a little and loosened out, and sure enough, there was the airfield right in front of us. Not only that, but it appeared there were lots of aircraft nicely lined up on the side of the grass strip, just waiting to be destroyed by our 20 mm and fifty calibre guns. We were, I thought, going to have a field day.

Well we did! But it wasn't quite as I had originally envisaged. The "enemy aircraft" turned out to be dummies (which became obvious as soon as we opened fire on them), and as we came back in frustration to wreak our vengeance on the buildings near the strip the whole area seemed to open up with anti-aircraft fire, and flak filled the sky. Neither of us was hit, but needless to say, we didn't waste any time fleeing the tempting target that had turned out to be nothing other than a flak-trap.

Our day was not yet over though. In the confusion and excitement of our flight from immediate danger, we got lost. Well, that was OK, because at least we were heading west, or so we thought. In truth, we were on a heading of about 340 degrees, and pretty soon as we were tooling along on the deck, our fuel getting low, and the weather getting worse, we began to get a little worried, since nothing familiar was showing up.

Suddenly, a landmark we couldn't miss appeared — the Zuider Zee! Hardly off course at all and deep in German-occupied Holland, but all of a sudden happy as two clams. Now we knew where we were, and the rest should be easy. Well, it wasn't too bad, although our precarious fuel state engendered a certain amount of sweat as we finally came upon B-88 Heesch and landed. Jack taxied in and parked, but I ran out of gas just as I approached the dispersal area. Needless to say, we both made tracks for the mess, where the bar was now open, and bought each other some cognacs (the only booze available).

February 7 may not have been a very nice day, but it was a pretty exciting one for me!

SIGHTED SUB — SANK SAME

Neil A. Burns, 442 Squadron

AFTER D-DAY, 442 SQUADRON was based at B-3 Landing Strip at St. Croix sur Mer, France, as part of 144 Wing. On the morning of July 8, 1944, 442 Squadron encountered an unusual target, even for us. We had been shooting up all kinds of locomotives, trucks, and bridges, but this was different.

We were on a beachhead patrol, four of us. I was in Y2-U, according to my logbook. We sighted one, and then two German mini-subs on the surface between Caburg and LeHavre. It was clear, and visibility was good, so those subs had no chance.

O'Sullivan in Y2-J, Wright in Y2-V, and Weeks in Y2-D and I dove down and shot up both of the subs. The first was damaged. The second was definitely sunk by the combined efforts of Wright and myself, five miles off Trouville, and we took pictures to show the intelligence officer.

Neil Burns of 442 Squadron.

Y2-P, PL 344, being restored to flight condition. This aircraft was flown by Neil Burns on a mission on October 28, 1944.

— Peter R. Arnold aviation photography

Later that day I flew to England to pick up a new Spitfire for 442 Squadron.

We continued with our usual targets after that. I did chase a 109 a few days later, but lost him. We also chased some of the jet Me 262s with limited success. Most of our work was rather routine ground attack and dive-bombing.

On October 6, 1944, the squadron was in a big air battle with 109s and 190s. I was in Y2-T, and got a big hole in my wing, so I was out of the fight early. But several of our pilots got scores, and I saw at least one 190 go down.

Another notable flight was on October 28. I was flying PL 344, Y2-P, when Don Goodwin (in Y2-G) flew a mission that made the papers. We were on a weather reconnaissance flight, when we encountered a perfect set-up for dive-bombing. Two trains were passing each other, and we scored direct hits on both of them, and on the way home we destroyed more rolling stock. Don Laubman nailed an FW 190 as we were attacking the trains. I was very pleased to find out from the author of this book that my aircraft from that mission still exists, and has been restored in 442 colours as Y2-P again for a museum in Florida. I hope to be reunited with my aircraft sometime soon.

Not too long after, on an armed recce, I was in Y2-S when I was attacking trains. I was shot down by flak, bailed out, and became a POW. So that was the end of my wartime flying. After the war, I was awarded a DFC for my service.

Buzz Bombs, Jets and Flak

Howard C. Nicholson, 402 Squadron

In AUGUST 1944, THE 402 SQUADRON received the Mark XIV Spitfire. We had only just gone over to Mark IXs in July, for a bit, and we regarded the Mark IX as a superior aircraft. The Mark XIV was not a whole lot faster than the Mark IX, but it was faster.

We went after the flying bombs the Germans sent over — very few people got the damn things. But those attacks did not last very long. By September 1944 we were in Nijmegen, flying fighter sweeps into Germany.

Looking at my photos, it brings to mind the fact that a lot of my buddies didn't make it. The flak was the worst problem. Nine out of ten guys that were killed were killed from the ground. By that time, though, we had air superiority, and the Germans didn't come up in any gaggles (of aircraft).

Except New Year's Day 1945. We got up and chased the rascals, as they had hit our airfield and killed quite a few fellows on the ground, including Vincent Denton Massey's son — he was an educational officer on the wing. The Germans took heavy losses too, and did not try that again!

There was not a lot of air combat, for most of our work consisted of going after trucks and trains on the ground. The XIV was a good aircraft, but could spin out. I can recall two of my buddies going after a train. I was flying top cover, and those two were going down. They made a violent turn to the right, couldn't hold it, and spun uncontrollably into the train.

By this time the shooting was a little hard to find. I did shoot down an Me 262, which was the first jet aircraft. I didn't really know what it was, but once I saw what it was, I whipped down on the damn thing and blew it away — my log says March 13, 1945, and my aircraft, a Mark XIV was AE-H. I had eleven or twelve fellows following me right behind, so I felt very brave — if the guy wanted to fight, it was an "even" fight (just kidding), but the Me 262 was hard to get!

I was interested to hear from a researcher in England recently that the pilot I shot down survived, but was injured in the crash.

Just as we were starting the last crossing of the Rhine, they sent me back to England. I was a little bit angry that I didn't get to stay until the last day, as I would have liked to stay on. I had been logging two hours and putting down twenty minutes, and they caught me! But my tour was up anyway.

We knew the war was over — it was just about finished with the crossing of the Rhine. There were thousands of planes and parachutists going in, and we just knew it was all over.

Spitfire XIV of 402 Squadron, AE-P, RM 727. — Hector Robertson photo courtesy J. Melson

Spitfires of 443 Squadron. — courtesy Greene

Groundcrew of AE-B "Emily," Brian "Blackie" MacConnell's aircraft.

FIVE EASY PIECES

Brian MacConnell, 402 Squadron

OUR BASE AT DIEST was just a farmer's field — it just happened to be smooth enough. It was an unusual set-up in one respect, in that it was basically a one-way landing strip — you could only land in a certain direction, because there was an orchard and trees at the other end, and there was a hill in the middle of it. So, you had to be pretty well stopped by the time you got to the top of the hill, or you gained on speed going down! The trick in landing there was to come in on your approach, and pull into a stall position. There was a fence on the edge of the field, so you'd look out the side, and when the fence passed under you, you dropped down. You then hopefully had enough runway so you could slow down, 'cause in a Spit, you couldn't brake very much, or you'd tip over.

After a few successful sorties with 402 Squadron I was starting to settle in, when, on December 18, 1944, I had a rather spectacular landing at Diest. We had taken off with belly tanks to escort some B 17s over Belgium. We climbed up to where they were supposed to be, but never did see anything, because there was cloud. So coming back this time with the belly tanks on (which added about 900 lb to the plane), I brought it in for a landing. I might have been a bit high, but anyway I pulled back on the throttle as soon as I saw the fence go by, instead of gliding in. I sort of dropped straight down, bounced up, came down, caught a wing, and then cartwheeled down, broke off both wings, the engine and the tail assembly. They were scattered down the runway in pieces, which was disconcerting. Anyway, it all stopped, and there I was, still strapped to the fuselage with nothing in front of me — no engine or instrument panel. I pulled the release, dropped a couple of feet to the ground, and went over to sit on the runway, looking back at the piece of aircraft. Oh boy!

Then the fire truck and the ambulance came out. When the ambulance arrived, the driver asked, "Where's the pilot?"

"Well, I'm the pilot," I said, to which he replied, "No, I mean the pilot of this aircraft."

"Yes, I'm the pilot," I repeated, and so he was finally convinced that I was the pilot — the guy who'd created this havoc on the runway.

My logbook shows I had been flying RM 849, AE-C, but now it was just a bunch of debris on the runway. The rest of the squadron was still in the sky waiting to come down. Eventually they cleared a path, and they got down OK.

Ken Sleep, F/Lt. of the flight I had been in, came along in a jeep and said, "Come on, get in the ambulance."

"I'm OK! I'm OK!" I said.

But he said, "You get in — we're taking you to the hospital."

"What's all this?" I asked, and he answered, "You may be OK, but if W/C Keefer gets you, you won't be!"

So I got stuck in the hospital for a couple of days with no visitors, particularly Keefer. He was in competition with all the other wing commanders, like Johnnie Johnson and the rest, for who had the best "for and against" record. Losing one of your own, even if it was an accident, was counted as "against," so Keefer was upset. When I came out of hospital I was shipped back to England for some bumps and circuits.

BRUSSELS FLYPAST

Lloyd Burford, 432 Squadron

On JULY 5, 1945, S/LT. DANNY BROWNE led 421, 443 and 416 Squadrons to Brussels. We were to be part of a large flypast of Mosquitos, Typhoons, Tempests, and Spits. The AOC (I believe it was of 83 Group, Second TAF) was leaving, and he was to take the salute when we flew past. We practised one day, and the next did the flypast, led by a wing of Mosquitos, which promptly missed the reviewing stand by about two blocks. They had navigators, too!

Next to them, second, came a wing of Typhoons, then our wing of Spits. The Mossies were flying about the right height, but they didn't give a damn about the Typhoons, who had to fly lower to miss the slip stream. And by the time we came and had to fly even lower, we were in the chimney pots. The Mossies missed, and the Typhoons followed, but Danny saw what was happening and changed course to be the first wing past the reviewing stand.

The following day, July 7, 1945, we had a day in town. That evening, of course, we drank a small amount. The next morning Chuck Lyons and I weren't feeling too good (same for the others, I'm sure), but we consoled ourselves by saying we'd be OK once in the aircraft, and turned on the oxygen.

Danny said he wanted us all on the runway together in twos, and we'd take off in formation as close as we could. I was number three, and feeling better, and Chuck and I gave each other the high sign. I was still not feeling so good as to take off

Lloyd Burford. — courtesy Burford

like that on such a short runway. Anyway, all went well, and I followed as soon as I saw that Danny was off OK.

It was a good trip back, but when the ground crew told us we didn't have oxygen in the tank when we left, we knew mind over matter sometimes worked!

Training days for Lloyd Burford in an older Spitfire.

This 403 Squadron Spitfire XVI, with red-white-blue spinner, takes off on a VE Day victory flight.

— RCAF official photo PL 45183

Spitfire XIV of 443 Squadron, postwar. — courtesy Shymko

W/C Geoff Northcott's Spitfire XIV.

Mark XVI Spitfires AE-Q and AE-T of 402 Squadron. AE-T was nicknamed "Refoogee II." — courtesy Melson

Spitfire XIV of 411 Squadron on postwar occupation duty.

Victory salute by aircraft of 84 Group, 2nd Tactical Air Force, with Spitfire XIV of 430 Squadron in the foreground, at Hengelo, Netherlands, on May 15, 1945. — National Archives of Canada PA 167603

The bad guys vanquished! Messerschmitt 109s and Focke-Wulf 190s at Schleswig airfield in May 1945. At the time, the Germans held out hope that these aircraft would be re-activated by the U.S. for war against the Russians.

— courtesy Beall

German 109s and 190s at Schleswig airfield in May 1945. — courtesy Beall

C/O Danny Browne and Adjutant Lloyd Hennessy of 421 Squadron have a look at a captured Ju188. — courtesy Beall

ACKNOWLEDGMENTS

Peter Arnold — Spitfire historian and owner
Bill and Shirley Austin — 402 Squadron

Almont Baltzer — Research and photos
"Barney" Barnard — 402 Squadron
Wilf Banks — 412 Squadron
Thomas Barton — transportation
Denes Bernad — aviation writer
Janice Beurling
Rick Beurling
Dave Boyd — 412 Squadron
Jack Boyle — 411 Squadron
R. D. Bracken — aviation research
W. J. Bracken — my father, with thanks
Cec Brown — 403 Squadron, for all his help
Lloyd Burford — 421 Squadron
Neil Burns — 442 Squadron
John Burtniak — Brock University

Lorne Cameron — 402 Squadron
Mike Carr — 414 Squadron
Norm Chevers — 403 Squadron
Ralph Clint — line drawings
Jim Curtis — research

"Chuck" Darrow — 416 Squadron
John DenOuden — RCAF
Mike Doyle — 411 Squadron

J. F. Edwards — 127 Wing, for his encouragement

Don F. Feduck — Research
Ed and Bea Ferguson — 443 Squadron
Hart Finley — 403, 416, 443 Squadron
Robert Finlayson — artist
Stephen Fochuk — aviation writer
R. D. Forbes-Roberts — 416 Squadron
Betty and Les Foster — 443 Squadron
Charlie Fox — 412 Squadron
Harry Furniss — 400, 442 Squadron

Monica Gomis
Harry Greene — 443 Squadron
George Greenough — 443 Squadron
Stephen Grey — Imperial War Museum
      Fighter Collection
Joe Gula — pilot

Bill and Dorothy Harper — 421 Squadron
Jack Harrington — Air Force Association
Victor Haw — 411 Squadron
Wally Hill — 416, 441, 443 Squadron
Tom Hitchcock — Monogram Books
Bill Hockey — 93 Squadron

J. E. "Johnnie" Johnson — Air Vice Marshall
— many thanks

Denis Keegan — Spitfire expert
Ian Keltie — 402, 442 Squadron
Bud Ker — 145, 402, 401 Squadron
Tim Knutson
Tommy Koch — 401 Squadron

Janet LaCroix — Canadian Forces Photo Unit
Paul Lewis — Polar Graphics Spitfire Decals
Ed "Lucky" Likeness — 412 Squadron
J. D. Lindsay — 403, 416 Squadron
Ron and Betty Lowry

John MacAuley — 411 Squadron
Dave McBride — 414 Squadron
Rick McGarry — photographic help
Barb McLay
Flo McPherson — research
Bill McRae — 401 Squadron
Ray Mills — 127 Wing Association devoted
    to veterans
Bob Morrow — 402 Squadron
Graham Moss — Imperial War Museum Fighter
Collection, Duxford
Jack Moul — 416 Squadron

Sue Newman

"Skeets" Ogilvie — 609 Squadron
Ian Ormston — 401 Squadron
Dick and Sylvia Ostronik — P 38 pilot

Loretta and Mel Pederson
J. B. Prendergast — 414, 430 Squadron

Stephen Quick — Stoddart

Bill Roberts — groundcrew
Jeff Robinson — research and photos

Art Sager — 416, 421, 443 Squadron
Wayne Scott — research
Pat and Rosa Simon
Howard A. Simpson — 402 Squadron
Dorothée Skalde — for all her help and
    encouragement
Larry Somers — 403 Squadron
"Hank" Sprague — 401 Squadron
Ann and Ray Steup

Garth Wallace — Canadian Owners and
    Pilots Association
Dwight Whalen — writer
"Duke" Warren — 165 Squadron
Cliff Whybra — aviation research
Roy Wozniak — 403 Squadron

"Stew" Young — 234 Squadron

Jan Zurakowski — 609 Squadron, Arrow pilot

And to the many others who provided access to
their logbooks and photo albums, and who took
the time to respond to my many questions.